ZANSHIN

FINDING THE POWER INSIDE YOUR DECISIONS

THOMAS KEYDEL

LEAP Portfolio Print, Publisher
Jamaica Plain, Massachusetts

ISBN: **978-1542363839**

Disclaimer:

Cover Art and Interior Illustrations by Michael Cucurullo
Cover Design by AnointingProductions

For more information about coaching services,
Go to www.tkeydel.com

Dedication

To my parents, family and life partner.
The only reason why we are in the world is to encourage a mutuality of love and support—
as best we can.

Contents

Acknowledgments

This has been an odyssey. There have been many readers of this manuscript (mostly in forms that are different from the one you now hold); to each person who helped me, I offer my gratitude and heartfelt thanks.

I must especially thank my sister, Janet Lawson; my mother, Roberta Keydel; and my good friend, Ken Orth; as well as my editor, Kelly Epperson; and my illustrator, Mike Cucurullo. Without the support of these unique individuals, this book would not have been written.

About the Author

Thomas Keydel, CPA, M. Ed. and GCEC

Tom is a Certified Financial Coach™ affiliated with Wealth Strong® and Fin Lab® financial services. He is a graduate of the Massachusetts School of Professional Psychology and has received training from CRR Global (Global Center for Right Relationship). Formerly a CPA and a Human Resource Trainer, Tom splits his time between writing and working with clients to develop greater awareness for their natural gifts and the larger contribution, which those gifts enable. Tom speaks to groups and organizations of all sizes and offers Zanshin courses to harness the power of decision making personally and professionally.

Website: tkeydel.com

About the Illustrator

Mike Cucurullo, Visual Artist and Illustrator

Mike is a classically trained artist specializing in helping people communicate visually. He has studied extensively in Italy, Holland and New York and has illustrated numerous books, internal corporate communications and visual presentations.

His commonsense approach to visual communication infused with passion, enthusiasm and a healthy sense of the absurd have been the driving forces in his 25-plus-year career as an artist.

His talents have been applied to toy and game development, concept sketches and whimsical social media blogs.

Website: cucurullo.com

About the Editor

Kelly Epperson, Ghostwriter and Editor

Kelly has written 30 books, some for New York Times best-selling authors, one that sold 3 million copies. She is a judge for the international Erma Bombeck essay competition. Kelly, a former IRS agent, is now an agent of joy, helping clients fulfill the goal of becoming an author.

Website: kellyepperson.com

INTRODUCTION

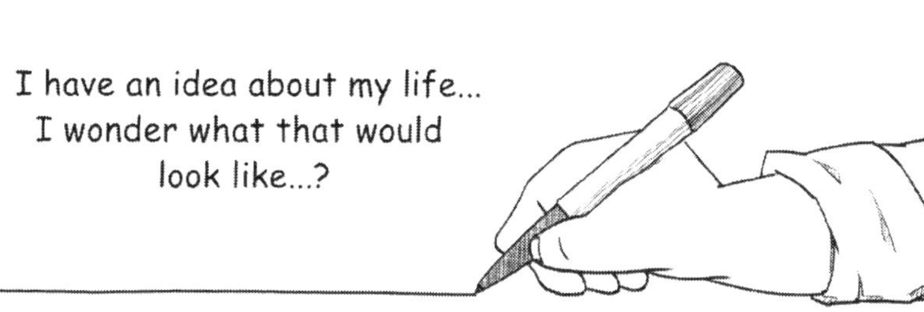

You are more than the person you have allowed yourself to be. The purpose of this book is to help you to reconsider how you operate and to help you better understand and harness your decision making power. Choice is more than an evaluation of options. It is a meeting place, a space you can use to discover yourself and the beauty of the world around you.

Don't be fooled by the cultural primacy of "reason" and its apparent logic. Your way of making decisions is not as cold, hard and immovable as you may believe. Between the "certainties" we build to fortify the rational walls of separation, there is *maybe*. Don't give away your maybes. Embrace them. Accept them. Make them part of you. The boundary between inner and outer is open, a beautiful complexity that only you can negotiate. Discovering and harnessing the openness of that boundary enables the unique person you are to flourish in ways you could never imagine.

The word *zanshin* is borrowed from the mindfulness techniques used by Japanese martial artists when sparring with an opponent. A "zanshin" fighter maintains an alert mental attitude before, during and after an action that is open and attentive throughout.[1] The more zanshin the fighters' approach, the more relaxed and focused their awareness becomes.

When we become zanshin, we realize the benefits of adopting an open and mindful approach to our decisions. A literal translation of the word, zanshin, is "remaining mind." Our decisions use not only the obvious and insistent demands of present experience, but also undisclosed experience, not directly found in the present. The "remaining mind" can be thought of as the latent ability to anchor one's decision making across conflicting points of view, some of which might run counter to one's conventional or immediate interests. Our ability to take up and use this remaining mind, to access the aggregate experience of those points of view that conflict with the demands of the present moment, diminishes as we become especially anxious or euphoric, or as we become especially preoccupied with self-promotion and how it claims our attention. Under extreme duress, we may even lose access to this ability altogether.

You know the phrase "in the zone"? The best way to conceptualize being zanshin is to think of it as being in the zone of optimal decision making. When you are "in the zone," you are not constrained by obstacles. *Maybe* becomes the risk you are willing to take because you can reassess, adapt and move on, no matter what.

Limits may seem insurmountable to you now, should you still be in the habit of approaching decisions from a perspective that is closed to considerations not present or manifest to you in the decision making moment. There is truly no clear delineation between right and wrong or success and failure. We put so much pressure on ourselves that every decision seems to weigh heavily upon our future. But who or what, really, determines *your* future?

- Is it the *gods* (or the one God) who brings you into contact with possibility and with limits?

---

1 "One arrow, one life: Zen, archery, enlightenment" by Kenneth Kushner; Tuttle Publishing, 2000, pg. 73.

- Is it *fate* (or inexplicable randomness)?
- Or is it *you* who creates (or at least shapes) your specific outcomes?
- Is it a combination of the three?

For many, "decision making" is another term for risk evaluation. What is the likelihood of a poor result? Of an outcome that represents loss, waste or ruin? We are consumed by risk evaluation, fixating on the risk and giving scant attention to any accompanying opportunity. Opportunity evaluation, in contrast, is a distant luxury to be contemplated only when there is something entertaining to decide.

Yet from a zanshin perspective, the evaluation of opportunity is more purposeful than the evaluation of risk. Opportunity leads; risk obstructs. To "succeed by failing" represents the zanshin shift that reorganizes and changes one's perception—making the place of discovery more valuable than risk or potential failure. By arriving at that place of unexpected discovery, a new appreciation is organized. We are not as limited as we believe: we can expand our options by letting go of the routine and familiar.

And isn't *that* what we long to realize?

To be zanshin, you must split your decision-making power equally among the three "forces" mentioned above, which I call *agencies*. Only by harnessing the force of these agencies in concert do you arrive at a decision: God/gods, in the form of Divine Agency; fate, or Impersonal Agency; and your own subjective experience, or Personal Agency. You can, at any time, shift the focus of your decision making among these agencies without becoming any less whole or complete as a result. For in truth, how can you be less whole than you are? You are a porous boundary, naturally complete, no matter how you evaluate and focus your decisions.

There have been multiple variables guiding and informing any decision you could make long before you considered focusing your attention on any one—so the zanshin moment and its remaining mind must precede what we think of as "organized reason." Otherwise the personal, impersonal and divine would be indistinguishable to you. How can the gods, fate or you be more "organized" than what you actually live through? Is it even "reasonable" to focus on just one?

So... Have there been multiple variables at play before you decided to read that newspaper?

To borrow from the irony of King Solomon's wisdom, this approach may seem to some like splitting the baby. Why three types of agency? What advantage could there be? Why deconstruct the benefit of "reason"? What's wrong with simply "being reasonable"?

Our dilemma is buried in the data. Do we look at what we are doing using a rational-empirical lens or an intuitive-spiritual one? Every decision offers you the chance to do either. So how do you decide?

You could employ Personal Agency. You could leverage your individual personality. "I am *that* **I am**," you say. Nothing else matters. You are aligned with and committed to your unique point of view and thus make decisions from there.

Another way would be to leverage the evidence. "**I am**—because there is '*other.*'" Only evidence matters. This is Impersonal Agency;

you are aligned with how things are given; you chalk the way life is up to fate.

Still another way would be leverage potential. "I am–**not** because I am, **or even** because there is 'other'—but simply *because life itself continues.*" What is "divine" in Divine Agency is the unfolding of whatever happens despite all expectation. Life continues. Nothing else matters.

A final way to approach your decisions would be to leverage the remaining mind, seeking its openness and flexibility as your primary refuge. This is zanshin. This is the power inside your decision. But why bother? Why remaining mind? Because you cannot direct your energy and attention towards the three agencies at the same time—you cannot bend your consciousness to be fully aware of all three at all times.

The most a zanshin warrior can achieve is one agency *plus* the remaining mind. Normally, our decision making is one agency *minus* the remaining mind. Too often we push out the remaining mind, thinking we must master one agency wholly, rather than balancing our approach between them all to optimize opportunities. But this does not work, and often reduces opportunities rather than expand them.

You see, the remaining mind is like a connecting tissue. It allows you to tap into the experience and emotion of all three agencies, even while you are attuned to just one.

To be zanshin, your commitment must be more deeply grounded than your tactics. The zanshin warrior operates on the conviction that *whatever unfolds* will confirm his deepest longing. The remaining mind as a storehouse of resilience unifies and integrates what the warrior's conscious mind cannot. The zanshin warrior allows himself to be drawn into a result that is larger and greater than his own particular and contingent expectation.

The zanshin warrior must be *willing* and *open* to whatever happens, no matter how he organizes or leverages his potential. The leverage is temporary, but the remaining mind and its capacity to integrate perspectives—that endures.

Those who are aware of how these agencies overlap will do better than those who are not. Everything has the potential to impact what you decide, so why be limited to just one or two agencies? Use all three!

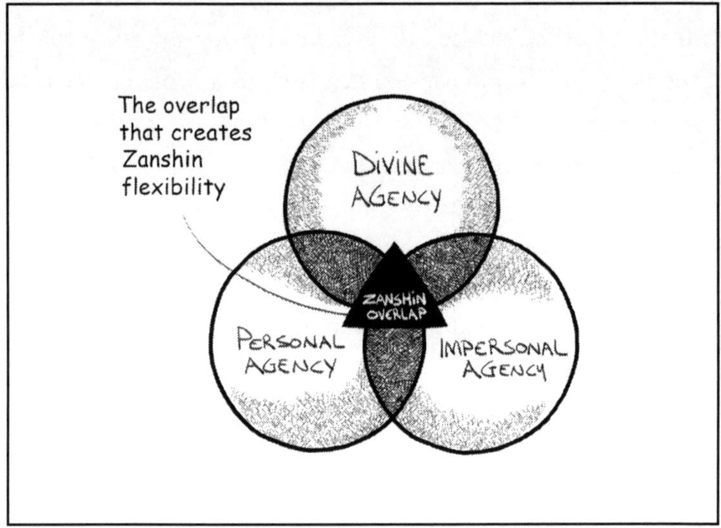

Some are adept at negotiating the boundary between personal and impersonal. They switch back and forth effortlessly. However, when life proceeds in a way that does not make sense, the personal side dominates. Self-determination replaces zanshin openness because they are no longer committed to the promise offered in the next moment.

Consider Joe. He was in a crisis: his wife left him. Flooded with emotion, Joe's desire for self-determination replaced his ability to negotiate the personal and impersonal. One agency *minus* the remaining mind limited Joe's ability to think impersonally—in an evidence-based way—about his wife's point of view. Identification with pain prevented Joe from considering how life might be trying to teach him something new. The Zanshin Overlap disappeared. All of Joe's actions were driven by the force of Personal Agency. Nothing else mattered.

Similarly, others negotiate the boundary between personal and impersonal by allowing the impersonal side to dominate. Here the reality of what is given feels larger than what they themselves might contribute.

Consider Sally. She, too, was in a crisis. As procurement manager, Sally's project was being derailed by cost overruns. Because she could not control what was being billed by her vendors, she spent weeks continuously following-up, never considering the toll it was taking on her time, energy and optimism. One agency *minus* the remaining mind limited Sally's ability to think more personally about what she was doing, or even how she might be preventing her company from accepting important information. The Zanshin Overlap disappeared. All of Sally's actions were driven by Impersonal Agency. She could not access the perspectives offered by Personal Agency or Divine Agency.

Still others are adept at negotiating the boundary between the personal and the divine by dissociating and separating from the impersonal. Belief dominates reality. The orthodoxy of what the next moment *should be* organizes perception. Here, personal action and impersonal cause and effect are seen as the expression of one "divine" perspective. As Voltaire's Doctor Pangloss might say, "all is for the best, in this, the best of all possible worlds."

Consider Steve. When his third marriage dissolved, he outwardly accepted responsibility for the split, but without acknowledging his own agency in what led to it. If this was what God required of him, then that was all that mattered. The truth of God's will could not be questioned, so whatever was personal or impersonal about Steve's particular way of relating simply didn't enter into his thinking. One agency *minus* the remaining mind limited Steve's ability to see that joy and happiness are shared in a fashion that cannot be ignored by hiding from the overlap of what is personal, impersonal and divine.

Each agency is partial and incomplete. Too much fidelity to any one of them can result in myriad decision making problems.

Too much ego results in self-interested self-determination. That is an excess of Personal Agency. Too much empiricism results in disconnection and helplessness. That is an excess of Impersonal Agency. Too much divine intervention results in a denial of responsibility for what happens. That is an excess of Divine Agency.

The problem with agency is trying to explain it. We want a *fully* conscious way of understanding ourselves inside the decisions we make, a way that integrates and holds all three agencies in a calibrated, harmonious tension. The zanshin perspective argues we cannot be fully conscious in this way. All three agencies are present; however, we can only give full credit and attention to one at a time as we move through them all.

Let's take an example. You are in an argument with your boss. You are taking the situation personally. The more your ego is implicated by her criticisms, the less flexible you become. The pressure feels overwhelming. While you stammer for control, your boss focuses on specific evidence, so you shift to the impersonal and try to reframe the situation as a collaborative partnership, describing each action taken and what they meant to you. Your boss recognizes this and does likewise. The moment unfolds and turns into an acceptance of mutuality that feels completely new to your relationship. Something has happened: in just a few seconds, you arrived at a place you never anticipated, an emerging understanding that feels larger than either of you alone. The surprise of Divine Agency is how unexpected it is. Shared mutuality doesn't enter into a relationship unless risk and opportunity are leveraged in new ways.

To explain why we have such difficulty acknowledging the situational leverage that each agency has, consider the following diagram:

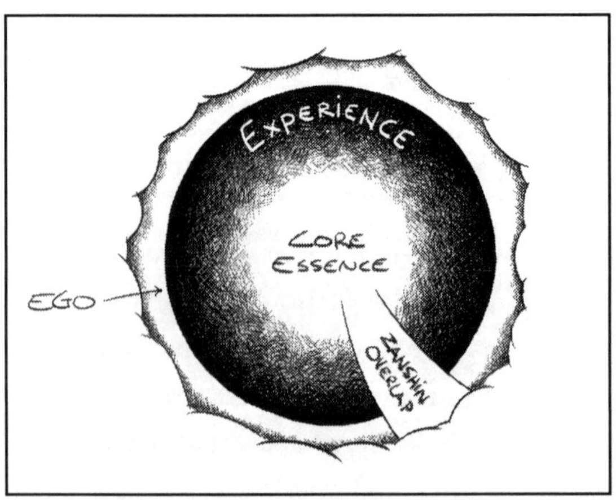

Core Essence is the sum total of your potential as it unfolds (via Divine Agency). *Experience* is your memory of how potential has played out in the past (via Impersonal Agency). *Ego* is the identity that you adapt and change (via Personal Agency). The situational leverage each agency has corresponds to the part that becomes most active. Your source of potential is your being alive and connected to the world as it unfolds. How your potential has played out for you is the intersection between you and everything around you as best as you can remember it. The identity you adopt is the protective barrier you create to safeguard not only the experience you have had but the future potential that may yet unfold—unexpectedly.

When we have a bad experience, Ego does its best to protect Core Essence; however, Core Essence uses everything we experience to confirm that which we might later choose to integrate. This ability to integrate implies that Ego and Core Essence are in a constant dance with lived experience being the music that creates both risk and opportunity. Based on what we accept and integrate or what we resist and disown, we can change the dance we are in—and only we can do this.

What we attend to—which can be Personal, Impersonal or Divine—*will be* most often one agency *over* the others. The most actively engaged agency influences our appreciation for what we are trying to decide, be that protection, discernment or confirmation.

The Venn diagram shown earlier illustrates the active parts in the decision making process: Ego protects; Experience discerns; Core Essence confirms. Each agency is integral, but frequently goes unacknowledged in the decision-making moment. Too much of one, and your decisions will be less effective. The situational risks and opportunities are not obvious if you evaluate everything based on the leverage created with just one agency. By using the *Zanshin Overlap*, Core Essence, Experience and Ego are given equal weight in whatever a person decides.

Let's take another example. You are frustrated with your spouse, who has different priorities in child rearing. You feel certain about what you want, and you know your spouse is less certain than you. Ego protects; Experience discerns; Core Essence confirms. Your spouse's indecision begins as ego protection. You are angry and fearful. As you gather new information, you learn that he/she prefers to give greater freedom to what the kids want to do; Experience discerns. New questions lead you to a range of alternatives: the family dinner is mandatory, but study habits can be negotiated. As you act on those alternative choices with confidence, Core Essence confirms. You and your spouse arrive at a place that holds the promise you want to share. Perfect knowledge is not required, because what unfolds is both larger and more complete than what each person started with. You have channeled all three agencies into your decision-making power without dwelling on any one in particular.

It is good to grasp the simplicity of "Ego protects; Experience discerns; Core Essence confirms." What these verbs point to is what we want from our decision making: protection, discernment and confirmation. However, we are highly prone to over-protect, over-discern and over-confirm, out of an exaggerated conviction to one agency or another.

The zone of optimal decision making can be difficult to understand—if we stubbornly resist setting aside the explanations that drive our moment-by-moment choices. We are *more* attached to the need that a selected agency expresses than we realize. Decision mastery cannot be understood by personal need, empirical need or situational need. The unfolding moment will move in an optimal direction, only if we choose to give each agency its due time in the limelight.

Consider the performance of star athletes like LeBron James, Michael Jordan, Simone Biles, Michael Phelps and Serena Williams. In the heat of the moment, the mastery they illustrate is not solely personal, impersonal or divine. It is a combination of all three driven by an unconscious but largely social desire that brings forward excellence.

What we create *collectively* is far greater than what we create *individually*. The Zanshin Overlap and the zone of optimal decision making is primarily a model of individual decision making and it *aspires* to be a model of collective effort as well.

The zone of optimal decision making responds to others. We do over-protect, over-discern and over-confirm. When angry or fearful, we are absorbed by the need of unfulfilled expectation. Anxiety and euphoria can force us out of the Zanshin Overlap. Every decision is, metaphorically, an act of self-promotion; however, with the Zanshin Overlap, we can teach ourselves to empty ourselves of any anticipated outcome and free ourselves accordingly. Indeed, this is why the remaining mind is so important.

Remember the classic Zen story about the master serving tea to a new disciple who could not stop talking about everything he already knew. The master continued to pour tea into the disciple's cup until it overflowed because the disciple was too full and could not empty out his own attachment. So too, each agency without the remaining mind is susceptible to becoming an overflowing teacup. We over-protect, over-discern and over-confirm by never allowing the remaining mind to empty us of our expectations and by failing to include others.

The Zanshin Overlap moderates our efforts by helping us to share the burden of protecting, discerning and confirming together which we can always do *with others*.

We must choose to coordinate. We must choose to express gratitude for decisions that rise above conflicting interests, priorities or dissimilar values. There is a "collective unconscious"[2] that expresses our collective striving in ways we do not appreciate; yet, the beauty of those strivings become "collective" the moment they cease to be representative of any one point of view.

Consider these examples of peak creation:

---

2 A concept put forward by Carl Jung to address the unconscious way of being that is shared among those who are moving to create a shared potential that is not specific to any one point of view. Here, a matrix of overlapping concern defines the "collective unconscious" rather than any one, predetermined outcome or result.

- The technical daring of scientists and engineers who overcame tremendous challenge to take human beings to the moon and back, who turned the antibiotic idea into a reality, who ushered forth the Great Wall of China, who performed the first heart transplant, or who discovered DNA.
- The stunning bravura of architects and artists who surpassed the standards and stereotypes of their day to create the Taj Mahal, the Forbidden City, the Statue of Liberty, the Cathedral of Notre Dame and the Mona Lisa.

None of these is just *an* expression of the personal, impersonal or divine. They are—all of them—larger than our conscious understanding of how these individual agencies work on us and through us. That's why, as examples, they hold such power to inform our decision making. We aspire to mix agencies so that whatever *is loved* finds a place beyond the limitations we label "failure," "strife," or "misery."

Being zanshin does not mean a simple averaging out of anxiety against euphoria to create a zone of optimal performance. Peak creation works by combining all three agencies so that we might actually learn to rise above our respective differences. Cooperation offers us the opportunity to be larger than ourselves by teaching us to set aside any excess self-promotion, especially around those perspectives that drive us to default or stalemating decisions, for surely, these decisions lead primarily to failure, strife and misery.

The life you save might be your own. Labels that blame and disparage are not indicative of the zanshin approach. The Zanshin Overlap blurs protection, discernment and confirmation by courageously allowing our decisions to include others as equals. Indeed, that is the joy we release by embracing and using the "collective unconscious" to protect, discern and confirm together.

Reinhold Niebuhr wrote:

> *Nothing worth doing is completed in our lifetime; therefore we must be saved by hope. Nothing true or beautiful makes complete sense in any immediate context of history; therefore we must be*

saved by faith. Nothing we do, however virtuous, can be accomplished alone; therefore, we are saved by love.

The zanshin moment is longer than a lifetime, more immediate than any context of history and cannot be realized alone. As important as our conventional, organized reason is—both for the evaluation of risk and for the appreciation of opportunity—every reason, rationale and explanation pales in comparison to *what we live through.* We are constantly sharing our deepest yearnings to love, and in the end, that sharing becomes both the explanation and the reason for every decision.

My Purpose in Writing

This book is part speculative philosophy and part self-help guide. The two do not always fit comfortably or well together.

The speculative philosophy part is much as you have already seen: a focus on what it means to be zanshin and the differing ways we can focus our decision-making power.

The self-help part is, perhaps, harder to appreciate. The needs that we seek to fulfill are as I have identified them earlier: to protect, discern and confirm. By exploring all three, we can appreciate the deep well that decision making represents. In the final analysis, every decision is an opportunity for self-exploration and self-promotion. That deep well is both a container and a reflection of how we accept the world and live through it.

The benefits you will get by reading this book are as follows:

- Make decisions with greater awareness.
- Access more positive energy with your decisions.
- Develop an empowering relationship with open-ended possibility.
- Reduce your fear of risk.
- Identify new choices and options with greater confidence.

- Be less pre-occupied by your decisions and more content with whatever happens.
- Free yourself from the grip of indecision.

The recommended techniques included herein are built around the needs we try to satisfy when making decisions:

- **Protect**—to identify and confront obstacles, pressures and fears that interfere with decision making. If we exaggerate these, we make our lives harder and we potentially put others at risk. A decision that protects need not *over*-protect.
- **Discern**—to question any automatic assumptions and to adopt an impersonal stance that can offer a greater insight. Past experience is both a source of constraint and a source of connection. What we want is greater connection, not greater constraint.
- **Confirm**—to offer consent and acceptance for the larger context we participate in, without defining that context too narrowly. Every expectation creates a desire for confirmation and not all can receive confirmation. What we want is a greater freedom to make our choices even though they are difficult to confirm.

By reading this book, the energy you put into these "verbs" will be less and your satisfaction greater.

My organization of material is as follows:

Chapter 1: Indecision Is a Problem. An examination of arbitrariness and what I call the "Utility Pendulum." If we want to make better decisions, then adopting a neutral outlook is useful. Every decision may appear arbitrary to others so a neutral outlook helps to create mutuality.

Chapter 2: The First Decision—Dealing with the Arbitrary. An examination of the three-part assignment we make when we protect, discern and confirm. Our first decision must be to set aside the urgency that those needs create, which means looking closely at how arbitrarily we assign needs to our experience. The world may go on without us arbitrarily, but we do not go arbitrarily on without others. Not if we are choosing cooperation. Setting aside urgency allows our awareness to deepen and expand, which helps us to make decisions more effectively.

Chapter 3: Personal Agency. An examination of why we protect ourselves from the risk of change. Using Buddhist wisdom stories, the difficulty of self-protection is explored and addressed. Self-protection is viewed as an extension of the reason, logic, appetite and spirit that express one's personality.

Chapter 4: Impersonal Agency. An examination of discernment and our desire for discovery. Here, the focus is on the six skills that can improve one's discernment. These include: enthusiasm, curiosity, empathy, imagination, processing feedback and negotiating with the unknown. Maybe becomes the risk you are willing to take once you learn how to be more effective with each of these skills.

Chapter 5: Divine Agency. An examination of confirmation and how it expresses a wish for spiritual connection. The safe space of being zanshin is the connection we feel to the remaining mind and how it resets our most persistent and troublesome, default expectations.

Conclusion. A look back at why decision making matters. Arbitrary systems may, in the end, betray us, but if we are zanshin "enough," we can hold on to what is most important and generate greater resilience and trust.

Wisdom stories are interspersed throughout the text to illustrate key points. Cartoons and illustrations provide light-hearted fun and offer visual rather than verbal avenues for approaching the book's content.

I do not specifically identify what you "must do" to make a better decision. Instead, I point to the broad areas that make decision making hard for us all and provide illustrating examples and exercises. The goal is to alter the way you arrive at your decisions, not to predetermine or sway your conclusions.

Obstacles, pressures and fears wreak havoc with our decisions. Untested assumptions impede and interfere, adding unnecessary complexity. A forced desire for an unchallenged confirmation is likewise a serious hardship. Yet despite these impediments, we *do* make decisions that demonstrate zanshin flexibility every day. My hope is that you see how interdependent and cohesive the three agencies are, and how they can be developed to reciprocally support one another. To protect, discern and confirm are distinct needs, yet every decision in some way must harness all three.

Arriving at Trust

In all the works of famous composers—in all the greatest music, song and dance—you will not find a single lie; for between composer and listener, there is no separation. The zanshin moment and its movement are not mysterious. Like a tree, it grows from its own unique seed, breathing life and shape from its promise of unbounded potential. The self-discovery that underlies our decisions is not easily understood. Yet there is a constant pressure to exclude or upend ourselves or others based on the discomfort or inconvenience we encounter. What we discover in such moments must counterbalance our wish to ignore or make light of the discomfort or inconvenience felt by others.

However, too often we are at a loss to make sense of what we *can* do together when opportunity and risk are so easily hijacked and distorted by the logic of individual agencies.

The loudness of our public reasoning masks a profoundly difficult problem: How do we arrive at trust? Decision making is a peak creation because it depends on trust. Nothing great is undertaken without trial, and nothing is more pathetic than unnecessary caution when everywhere there is growth and change—all without the benefit of "reasoned" explanation and without resistance.

When we embrace growth and change, every important decision is drawn upward into the sky—like trees or mountains or the feathered wings of eagles. Our decision-making power is, itself, like an open-ended sky with a canopy of stars flowing everywhere without explanation. We can learn to have greater trust.

Since my avowed purpose is to have you reconsider the primacy of reason, know now that *what is zanshin* cannot be fully explained. Like beauty, it is drawn upward, remaking the world entirely without explanation. The zanshin moment is offered and you are invited—but you must reach for it.

Alan Turning famously argued that intelligence can be evaluated by how it is imitated. The more convincing the imitation, the more likely it is that intelligence may be inferred. However, being zanshin is not about imitating a certain kind of intelligence, for no two people are ever alike. The zanshin ideal is about giving ample room to the remaining mind, for only by gaining access to its latent potential can the most human qualities be realized: patience, loving-kindness and equanimity. It isn't just that protection, discernment and confirmation are the "verbs" we chase after when arriving at a decision; it's how we use all three at the same time. That latent potential is what enables us to hold on to hope and build for ourselves the enlarging belief that we can be more together than alone. The vulgarity of human expression, whether in thought, belief or action, results whenever we distort our sense of need, and that happens most often whenever we under appreciate what we already do share with others.

Unlock the potential of your decision-making capabilities. The rationality of reason is necessary, yet the upward movement of growth and change is the larger and more expansive awareness to which you are invited.

The gods (or the one God), Fate (or inexplicable randomness) and You (with your impassioned mind) are all participants in the zanshin moment. As Rumi wrote, so is the essence of zanshin:

"Beyond ideas of rightdoing and wrongdoing there is a field. I'll meet you there."

In the traffic pattern that organizes our everyday lives, it is sometimes hard to figure out what's right or wrong, even when we wait patiently off on the side.

Hey! What's with the lights - are they stop or go?

Framework

The conceptual framework this book offers is based, in part, on Reivich & Shatte's *The Resilience Factor: 7 Keys to Finding Your Inner Strength and Overcoming Life's Hurdles.* It examines what the authors identified as the "personal, permanent and pervasive" assumptions that undergird the relationships we maintain. The significant advance offered by this book is to amplify and operationalize that idea so that we can see more clearly how our choices and decisions are simply the extension of what those assumptions create, and how we continuously update and change them every time we add fresh experience and challenge.

CHAPTER 1:

Indecision Is a Problem

CHAPTER 1:
Indecision Is a Problem

Monumental forces and arbitrary forces are hard enough to work with, but once the tent of coordination begins to collapse, it's really hard not to wind up feeling like a clown. Monumental forces are the natural ones like environmental, physical or biological. Arbitrary forces are the man-made ones like economics, culture and politics. The tent metaphor assumes that with coordination, mankind can be independent of both. However, indecision is a problem because it draws away the power we need to coordinate together.

Everyone experiences indecision, including the frustration and loss of power that accompanies it. Yes, loss of power.

This book's primary question is: *What is the power that is inside your decisions?* That power comes from choosing to be zanshin.

When you are zanshin, your appreciation for power changes. You start to see that it arises from inside *of you*. Instead of responding to arbitrary and monumental forces as if they are on the outside, you begin to take control of them from the inside.

When in the grip of indecision, we sometimes behave like clowns. Our awareness for the true source of power waffles. It's like flipping a coin where the other guy says, "Heads, I win. Tails, you lose." You're not sure *why* it's wrong, you just know that it is.

To be zanshin is a paradigm shift. We are accustomed to outcomes. Yet, as you will see, they're not ideal. Outcomes force our hand by making us believe that we cannot decide for ourselves. Outcomes take away our power. If we give ourselves room to appreciate the relationship we are having, we gain freedom. Our relationship to power is always greater than its outcome. Even knowing this, we still measure our decisions based on the desirability of outcomes. We simply enjoy being like clowns.

Let's take for example the uber-gameshow, *Who Wants to Be a Millionaire?*™ The contestant is facing a gigantic opportunity, a chance to win ONE MILLION DOLLARS!

The big money question IS:

In the children's book series, where is Paddington Bear originally from?

a. India
b. Peru
c. Canada
d. Iceland

Now to some, this decision might be mindlessly easy. They have the right information and know what to do right away. They are certain. Others will feel completely lost. Unable to decide, these participants will replay the opportunity and risk. The outcome is now two-fold: either ecstasy or humiliation. The fact that their indecision is driven by an all-or-nothing outcome makes it twice as hard to decide anything.

The show's "lifelines" are, of course, a sanctuary for the indecisive. Your potential options include: "50-50" (eliminate all but two answers); "Phone-a-Friend" (depend on someone else's judgement); or "Ask the Audience" (poll the masses for their answer). Suddenly there is a midpoint between ecstasy and humiliation. You actually have something you CAN do. It's not just about the two unavoidable results.

Suppose you use the "50-50." Your options are reduced to:

a. India
b. Peru

Now your mind is spinning. You are previewing all the justifications that seem to make one answer better than the other. You have no certainty with regard to your answer so the justifications seem light and ephemeral. You could just as easily be wrong as you could be right. Your mind fixates on the statistics: you have a 50-50 chance! That's just a coin toss. But a 50-50 chance is still ecstasy or humiliation. The result seems contradictory and impossible. You can't possibly be both at the same time. The result is never going to be a combination of the two. Logic won't let it. The excruciating pain stems from how impossible the situation feels. You are completely and utterly indecisive. Now your only wish is to get this over with as quickly as you can.

You close your eyes. You remember that Paddington Bear wears a blue raincoat. You decide that feels "English" to you. You know that India was a British Colony. Final Answer: A. India. The host of the show, Regis Philbin, asks you again, "Is that your final answer?"

Ecstasy or Humiliation? Justification or Loss? Right or Wrong? The stakes couldn't be higher. You courageously answer, "Yes. That's my final answer."

The room goes silent as you sit through the show's interminably long wait. The buzzer sounds. Wrong answer.

The lightheaded wish for all the possibility and joy of becoming a "millionaire" suddenly drains out of you. You are now on the other side of the moment, and you have lost! And you remember you are in front of millions of people. What humiliation!

But then.... your internal dialogue begins. *Nothing really happened. I am fine. It's only a TV show. I really didn't have any idea what I would have done with all that money, even if I had won it. I'm still the same.* Your perspective suddenly turns from overinvested to uninvested.

So what's going on here?

The result that was driving your adrenaline was something you could let go of; the result you got, while not wished for, is still OK. When you go back to the office, you will be a minor star for the day, a person with a vibrant story that makes you unique and different from everyone else, but you are still going to fit in, more or less, the same way you always have. Your life goes on. The brinksmanship experience only makes "real" how arbitrary things are. Yes, you could have said "B. Peru." But you didn't. So why, then, did you put yourself through that rollercoaster of emotion? Relations.

What we extend through time and what are always changing, are the subtle but important relations we have with the past, present and future. The clearer we are about *who we are* in those relations, the greater our freedom to take risks—even when the outcome is entirely arbitrary and completely unknown.

Decision making is *not* about the environmental swirl that takes place on the outside; *it is the constancy of who we are in the relations we have that matters.* When you understand that, you will become more decisive. Your need to protect, discern and confirm will stay with you. You will be freer and more zanshin about everything that happens.

The benefit of being zanshin is that you can bring forward your best and highest self by contributing more and feeling better about it. The zanshin shift is about sustaining a relation that does not change—unless you want it to. As contradictory as that seems while fixated on the ecstasy or humiliation of potential outcomes, that is the point. Be open, uncommitted and relaxed. Let your life be more happy and fulfilling, and what's more, it's entirely an inside job! The constancy of who you are is between *you* and *you*. The rest of this book will lead you to that conclusion. It's a journey you won't want to miss.

Agency? What Is That?

Fire sale, everything must go.

This book focuses on developing a zanshin approach by learning how to shift the agency that you use when making a decision. To be zanshin is to split the means of your decision equally among Personal Agency, Impersonal Agency and Divine Agency—without deciding you are any less whole or incomplete as a result.

"Agency" sounds like a fancy word, but it's not. To be an agent is to act on the basis of your power and to give it focus. Each agency is simply a different way to focus power. The more deftly you can switch between the three agencies, the more zanshin you will become.

Consider these obstacles that we frequently encounter when trying to make a decision; these will help us why agency is so important.

1. Incomplete Information. Here, we lack the right information. Our options are not fully identified and we cannot get behind any one option.

Suppose you want to meet a friend, but your friend has not been clear about the time to meet. You are also situationally aware that this friend has been having a difficult time at home and at work.

On the one hand, you reason: This is a long-term friend and the meeting might be relevant, yet you are not sure. You think: *It's worth the risk to hold a place in my appointment book because my friend is important.*

In contrast, you also reason: This is a limited opportunity, nothing is clear, and this is more risk than I want. You think: *I don't want to waste my time.*

Without enough information, you are torn between protecting your friendship or protecting your time.

2. Lack of Priority or Conflicting Priorities. Here, you have enough information and your options are clear; however, you cannot decide between contrasting priorities.

Suppose you have two relatively clear options: Either you move to a new city to take a new job, or you stay where you are and keep working where you have been. Of course, the variables are hard to figure out because you cannot determine what exactly might happen.

On the one hand, you reason: The move is a one-time event but brings with it a long-term effect, the money and responsibilities are great, and you have a great sense of hope. You think: *It's worth the risk.*

In contrast, you also reason: The move is permanent; you will stop seeing your friends and co-workers here, and you're not sure about that. You think: *The social risk is more than I want.*

The priorities here are professional and social. With so much left to be experienced once you make your move, it's hard to know which priority might give you the greatest payoff, so getting real with any potential loss requires a high degree of discernment.

3. Conflicted Feelings from the Past. In this case, your options moving forward are all tied to the past. The moment is not altogether new. It is *deja vu* all over again.

Suppose your current boyfriend is hedging his commitment to you, just like your last boyfriend did. Either you decide the current situation is entirely different from the past, or you accept its apparent similarity. However, the variables are painful because that memory is painful.

On the one hand, you reason: It happened *with* the previous boyfriend and it's over, you survived and learned something. The future can be whatever you want to make of it. You think: *No, my current situation is not about the past.*

In contrast, you also reason: Your current boyfriend's hedging might continue, you don't really know what it means, and you don't want to risk repeating the same thing. You think: *Yes, this is just exactly like the past.*

The conflict you are feeling arises from your history and from your boyfriend's behavior, so it's hard to know where to place your loyalties.

The past is the past and yet sometimes, it repeats.

All three obstacles presented above require you to focus your energies and move towards a decision. When you are zanshin, you will have three alternative paths.

To be zanshin is to travel down any one of three paths. With experience, your ability to do so will be based on intuition and feeling, not on thinking. Whether we know it or not, most of our decisions are "pre-decided," that is, we already have a clear sense of what we want and are simply looking for the rational justification that explains what we want.[3] This is why ecstasy and humiliation loom so

3 The psychologic research of Benjamin Libet (1916-2007) highlighted how unconscious neurological processes precede conscious decisions to perform both volitional and spontaneous acts. Most of these decisions come from unconscious preferences that are waiting for a rationale.

vividly out in front of us: we want to trust them and incorporate them because we are not sure that we can *be* worthy or meaningful without them.

Outcomes are exhilarating because they have the potential to protect, discern and confirm what feels "decided" by us already. With a zanshin approach, you can refine your pre-decisions so you don't have to suffer the arbitrariness of either ecstasy *or* humiliation. Surprisingly, you don't have to make decisions based solely on outcomes.

Every pre-decision, however, can potentially make our decisions harder, not easier. When a decision feels "pre-decided" in more than one way, it's likely we will rationalize our indecision. Since the three paths satisfy the decision maker in different ways, the way you rationalize a pre-decision depends on the satisfaction you are trying to realize. All three agencies offer valid rationalizations, which is why we are so easily tripped up by indecision.

The following diagram outlines the most important features associated with each agency. These are discussed below.

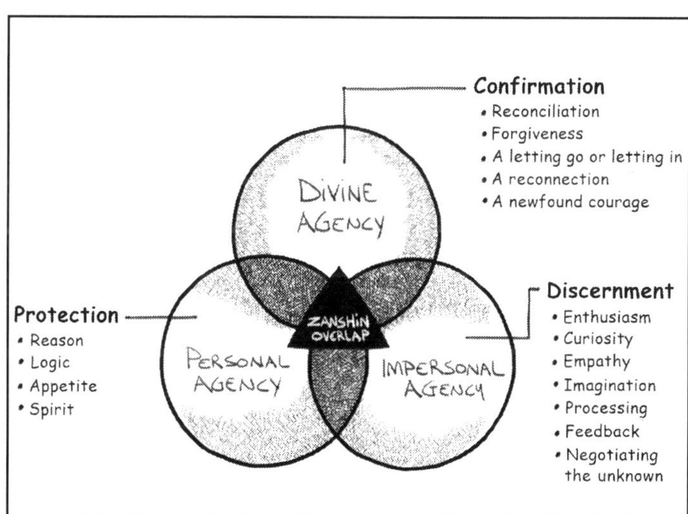

Personal Agency focuses on *protection* and personality. What you want to protect is at least partially determined by personality. As the possessor of reason, logic, appetite and spirit, the way you express your personality is to protect it from outcomes you do not want and to seek outcomes that you do.

Since Personal Agency looks forward to *outcomes*, this is often the hardest agency to manage. When we are zanshin with Personal Agency, we make a conscious choice to look at our habits and defaults *before* we engage with outcomes. Only by prioritizing the relations we want, can we free ourselves from the burden of over-protection. This perspective coordinates with many Zen Buddhist teachings and in future chapters, I draw upon several wisdom stories from that tradition.

Example: The "Incomplete Information" scenario above asks for Personal Agency. You must adopt a Zen-like distance when negotiating around incomplete information. What you learn from being zanshin is that there is no right or wrong decision, only how you feel about the relation with your friend and ultimately, the relation you have with yourself. Here, you are deciding how much protection is necessary.

Impersonal Agency focuses on *discernment* and explanation. Impersonal Agency can be compared to *fate* (or inexplicable randomness). We are given what we explain. The more we can accept fate as a potential explanation, the more we can move to examine all explanations without fear.

With Impersonal Agency, we are engaged not with outcomes, but with six different skills: enthusiasm, curiosity, empathy, imagination, processing feedback, and negotiating with the unknown. By sustaining an optimistic and forward-looking focus, we can examine the various choices and options with greater awareness and neutrality. Impersonal Agency focuses on discernment, but only after we let go of any need to protect. Only then, can we look at all possibilities equally.

When using Impersonal Agency, we must presume there are *unknowable* reasons for everything that happens, so what commands our attention is how we use the six skills without trying to shape a prescribed outcome or explanation. Personalizing emotions, such as fear and joy, are secondary to what we discern.

Example: The "Lack of Priority" scenario asks for Impersonal Agency. Here, we are discerning a priority. That priority may be moving for the new job or it may be staying put. Here again, a Zen-like distance clarifies our engagement. Once we can see that there is no right or wrong discernment, we can relax without trying to nail down a specific outcome or even explanation. The six skills, as we use them, will generate flexibility, thereby leading us, indirectly, to discernment.

Divine Agency focuses on *confirmation* and acceptance. Since life unfolds through an undisclosed energy that is unknowable to us, we have only a limited appreciation for how we are being shaped. Divine Agency focuses on confirmation, but only after we stop trying to discern or protect. Here, the acceptance which we bring to Divine Agency expands our decisions by confirming our connection to Core Essence. With greater acceptance of that, the confirmation we are looking for arises naturally without being forced and with that confirmation, we are likely to find new resources leading to greater resilience and strength.

With Divine Agency, we are engaged not with outcomes and also not with skills; Divine Agency asks us to look more closely at the person we want to become. The tension between Impersonal Agency and Personal Agency is largely about discovery. If we were to make a decision and take action, what might we discover about ourselves?

In contrast, Divine Agency is about resetting the confirmations that occupy our attention because we have already made some discoveries previously. To be filled with zanshin energy is to bring forward the "secure ground" of who we are and what we are being called to do regardless of any prior awareness or expectation.

In Chapter 5, the transitional actions that lead to greater strength and resilience are covered. These include: to reconcile with and forgive others, to let go or to let in an unpleasant consequence, to reconnect with the past, or to discover a newfound resolve for a specific mission or goal.

Example: The "Conflicted Feelings with the Past" scenario most clearly calls for Divine Agency. With Divine Agency, the person we want to become will always be larger than the person we have been in the past.

I'm pairing the three agencies with the three scenarios mostly to introduce to you the various terms that will be used throughout this book. These pairings are, for the moment, general applications. This loose understanding will change as you learn more.

Every decision combines the secure ground of who we are and what we are called to do but only if we freely blend together the Personal, Impersonal and Divine without over-investing. To protect, discern or confirm a "pre-decided" expectation may feel comfortable and right, but it often minimizes what we can achieve.

Stick with me; it gets clearer as we go.

Each agency works off a trigger. Protection, discernment and confirmation are trigger needs that focus our attention. When you are strongly invested in what's happening, you are triggered by what you "pre-decide." For ease of understanding, I use the terms "ME" and "NOT ME" to look at what we are pre-deciding.

The trigger preferences that you WANT to take possession of are called "ME preferences." These are feelings you desire. These situations will make you feel lighter, more enabled and more connected to the world around you. Simply put, these are what you (the decision maker) want to make part of your life.

You also have trigger preferences that you want to RUN AWAY from. These situations will make you feel heavier, less enabled, and more cut off from the world around you. These I call "NOT ME preferences" because you (the decision maker) want to reject and resist these feelings or situations.

The "ME preferences" are triggered by feelings of.....

- Safety
- Peace
- Being respected
- Belonging and inclusion
- Success
- Bravery
- Affirmation
- Consolation
- Capability, even superior
- Confidence
- Acknowledgement
- Happiness
- Comfort
- Being desired
- Trust and support
- Wholeness and completion
- Being understood and seen as "right"

The "NOT ME preferences" are triggered whenever you feel .....

- Afraid
- Angry
- Dismissed
- Disrespected

- Excluded and not belonging
- Failure
- Fearful
- Humiliated
- Hurt
- Incompetent and inferior
- Insecure around others
- Lonely
- Sad
- Shut out
- Ugly, dirty or undesirable
- Unsupported
- Denied justice
- Broken or incomplete
- Misunderstood and seen as "wrong"

Your ME and NOT ME pre-decisions influence your decision-making ability. They make the current moment tangible and real, and they stand as automatic, unquestioned predictions about the possibility of future hardship or pleasure. You will probably find it difficult to shake off the feelings that either set of triggers create because they are strongly coordinated with anxiety, which we don't want, or euphoria, which we do.

One way to think about these contrasting feelings and triggers is to imagine a pendulum swing. Those feelings and triggers you want (ME) are on one side. Those you do not want (NOT ME) are on the other side. Everything that happens in your life will cause you to swing between these two states.

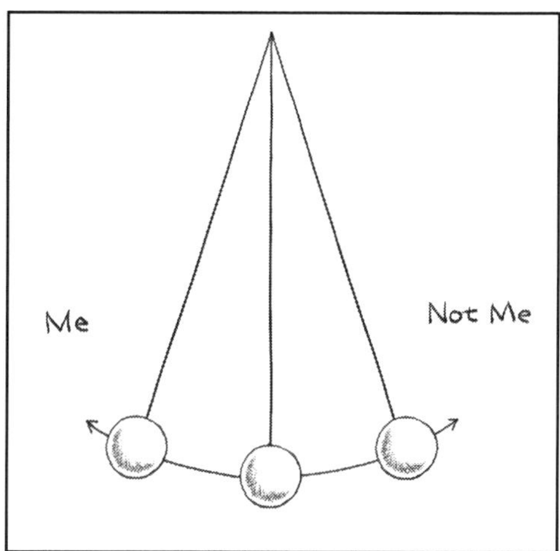

By making a decision, you are looking to generate "decision utility," that is, you are trying to protect, discern and confirm what you want to do next using the personal, empirical, and situational pre-decisions you have right now.

How Life Gets "Sewn into Time"

To be zanshin, you must discover how life events get sewn into time. The trigger responses you have get sewn into time by the way you match a remembered trigger with a decision utility. Indeed, the cornerstone to becoming zanshin is that you can change those trigger preference and reset the need those preference are trying to express.

With every moment, you are recording what happens based on the preferred feeling it generates—or not. Everything you live through gets embedded into your brain's neurological pathways and affects how you make decisions going forward. How you felt *through* and thought *about* something that happened in the past affects the decisions you are likely to make today.

The way you record these impressions (and act on them) requires a three-part evaluation scale. The three parts include:

- **Duration** (or **Durability**)—How long might this event last—is it permanent or temporary and passing?

- **Scope** (or **Importance**)—How deep is the impact of this event—is its importance "universal" or just particular and specific?
- **Preference** (or **Preferential Feeling**)—Does this seem like a ME event or a NOT ME event? Are you drawn to it and want it to last longer and be part of you? Or do you want to dismiss it and throw it away as quickly as possible?

The more you seek to protect, discern and confirm the responses you already have, the more you will try to support these initial impressions. The length, breadth and depth which these impressions create (as duration, scope and preference) get "sewn into time" and will pre-decide how we are likely to think and feel as we move forward.

Let's say that your boss made a cutting remark that you take personally. The feeling is clearly NOT ME. Your preference would be to throw it away as quickly as possible. Your immediate impression is to see this as a repeat of an earlier experience. The fact that the current event is so similar to *that* experience and *to other experiences* when you were criticized leads you to feel that the scope is universal. This upsetting event is both relevant and important to you. While its duration might be temporary, the energy that is unleashed lasts longer than the event itself. So the duration, as a remembered event, lingers and extends, making you feel that your relationship with your boss has shifted permanently. The permanence of this event is that *it actually happened.* So now the duration and scope you assign start to share a reciprocal energy, reinforcing the NOT ME feeling that leads you to react in a certain way. The length, breadth and depth of this event (as duration, scope and preference) can feel empowering but also enslaving. It's difficult to work around the immediacy of these pre-decisions and how they impact us. Sometimes they are useful, often they are not.

We will practice making these evaluations at the end of this chapter; however, from this example I hope you can see how lived experience gets sewn into time based on the duration, scope, and preference that we assign. Past and future awareness is most often organized by these self-generated impressions which, in turn, enable us to promote our particular interests because they cause us to think and react both with greater integrity and with less flexibility.

The way we record and play back these unique impressions serves to contextualize our values, personality, and perhaps, even some aspect of our "species" awareness (collective unconscious). A pre-decision is not just a feeling; it's a pattern of thought that brings together both past and future awareness. That preferential feeling becomes an impetus for whatever utility our decisions might realize—that is, to protect, discern or confirm the relation we are constructing for ourselves and others.

Ego protects; Experience discerns; Core Essence confirms. Pre-decisions arise to focus our attention in specific ways, and because they are different, that creates the potential for indecision. An impulse to protect draws on a specific way of relating to what we notice, thus making it harder to discern or confirm anything that might alleviate that initial impulse to protect.

Perhaps the duration, scope and preference evaluations seem complex. I encourage you to see them as scaling impressions that enable us to be energetically involved. These evaluations allow us to move from past to future awareness so we can make claims and organize our efforts. To some, these evaluations might be too general or inexact to be useful. That may be, but you wouldn't have manageable impressions of what you actually live through without them.

The utility we realize with each decision is largely a product of the permission we give ourselves to accept or challenge whatever we notice. Our specific way of relating harnesses what we live through by permitting inferences to first enter and then sway our awareness. The greater our awareness of that permission, the greater our ability to harness what power we have—without being enslaved by it.

Arbitrariness and the Utility Pendulum

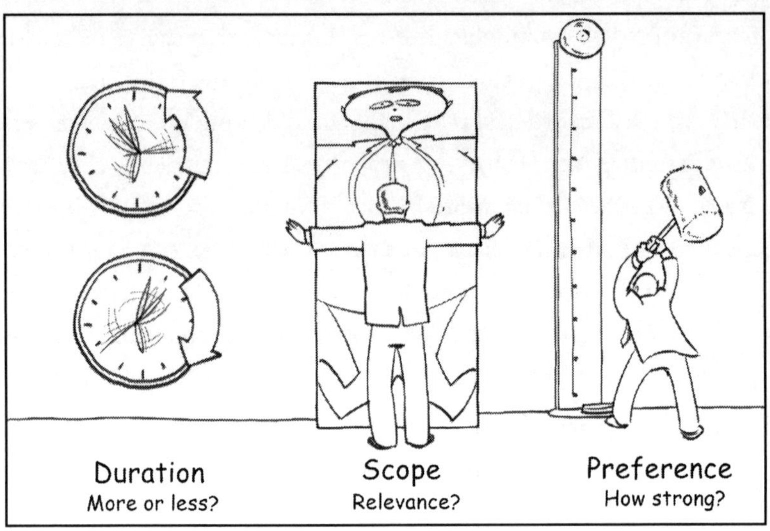

Exaggeration is a weird type of enslavement. When we exaggerate duration, scope and preference, we test the impact that a situation has on us. Of course, every situation has a felt duration (slightly more or less), a felt relevance (an inaccurate mirror we must use anyway), and a preferential feeling (a feeling that rises and falls with conviction). The more strongly we feel pushed into or pulled out of our reactions, the more harshly we may judge ourselves or our situation.

Because we do make snap decisions based on our pre-decisions, the world can seem a bit arbitrary. It might even seem to swing wildly back and forth in contradictory ways. Exaggeration makes it hard to limit the impact a situation has on us.

When indecision strikes, we are grappling with fear, mostly about some consequence or result. We are still very outcome oriented - ecstasy or humiliation? Every fear begins with the ME | NOT ME tug of war. That tug of war will hamstring us if we base our every action primarily on outcomes. If we want to be more zanshin, we must prioritize the relation we are having by giving room to *inter*dependent opportunity rather than exaggerated outcomes that only we care about. Letting go of outcomes and stepping into relation is the one shift we must make if we are to disengage from the ME | NOT ME tug of war.

That shift towards openness and neutrality creates the zanshin moment. Too often we associate decision making with rational evaluations. We survey evidence, make claims, organize our decisions and take action based on what we believe is useful or beneficial. What we do not recognize is that most of our evaluations are self-generated. The lesson of mindfulness meditation is that we learn how self-generated those evaluations are. We can intervene to alter that perception and open it to investigation. Indeed, that is what this book strives to do.

To arrive at a more zanshin preference, we cannot be enslaved by what we pre-decide. Exaggeration will only lead us to view the world more narrowly. To move past that, we must revisit duration, scope and preference so they can be more preferentially inclined to the relation we want and then allow that relation to be both worthy and truthful for us.

The beauty of being zanshin is that you never lose *your* power. The more attuned we are to how we shape those evaluations *preferentially,* the more we can visualize the relation that we want, without giving away our power to unknown, and frequently inconsequential, outcomes.

The challenge is realizing how every *self-created preference* is a three-part impression linked to a habitual way of thinking and being. The more resistant and guarded we are, the more energy we give to probability and outcome. To become zanshin, we must unlearn old habits and begin new ones. We must let go of arbitrary and unexpected outcomes and create a more enduring relation. If we move to blunt the extremes in the ME | NOT ME tug of war, then a new potential is created—a more zanshin potential.

To visualize this shift, consider the following diagram:

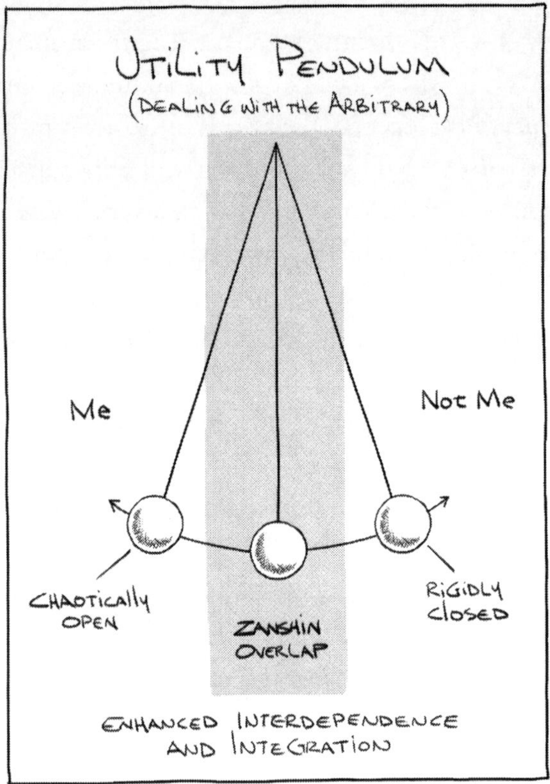

I've titled this the "Utility Pendulum" to emphasize that *at no time* is there just one outcome. Utility is never a result. Utility is a more complete rendering of the fulfillment that comes with greater interdependence. The more you focus on a relation (rather than an outcome), the greater your fulfillment. *The objective is to stay in the area of the Zanshin Overlap.* Doing so allows you to change old habits and maximize the utility of your future actions. There you will realize enhanced interdependence and integration without becoming enslaved by what you pre-decide.

Does this diagram imply that you must remain open and neutral to every decision? No. However, the risk of having *too great* an investment is that you might make "snap" decisions based on an exaggeration. Self-promotion and utility we are tied to duration, scope and preference. The more chaotic or rigid our exaggeration, the more enslaved we will become.

The subtitle "Dealing with the Arbitrary" indicates that by avoiding a triggering extreme, you can let go of any compulsion to act precipitously, and therefore, include others in your decision-making process. Given the conflicting needs used to focus a decision we might not always understand what we were doing or how much we are implicated by what we are deciding. Indeed, this is why arbitrary action feels so unsettling and why satisfaction is so difficult to realize. Self-promotion exaggerates our sense of need, thus leading us to feel put upon by others.

The label "enhanced integration" means tolerating ambiguity while "enhanced interdependence" means trusting others to share the moment with you. The "chaotically-open" and "rigidly-closed" indicators will be discussed later in the upcoming section.

There is no shortcut. Too much reliance on exaggerated outcomes makes the life we share that much harder to maintain or to enjoy.

Banishing the Arbitrary

The *arbitrary* is the outcome we did not choose or the outcome we chose without fully knowing it. The two extremes illustrated by the pendulum swing help us to visualize the arbitrary forces that cause us to feel unnecessarily challenged by others.

To leave the arbitrary behind, we must orient to a relation, rather than an outcome. The best is yet to come because the exaggerating effects of Personal, Impersonal or Divine agency can be left behind. Indeed, that is why the Middle Way is so compelling. It leads to a different style of celebration. Why else would you want that party hat?

If we do not orient to a relation, we will gravitate towards a much more exaggerated proxy: *an outcome.* With so much on the line and with *only an outcome* to define our place in the action, we become anxious or euphoric trying to protect, discern and confirm the path we want while at the same time holding in the strong feelings about what the outcome might be specifically for us.

The self-promotion realized by wanting one particular outcome causes us to become anxious or euphoric in unexpected ways. Indeed, this can feel like a Pandora's Box, leading us to become ever more enslaved by our wish for self-promotion.

For example, when an unexpected outcome opens a Pandora's Box of exaggerated reward, we ride a wave of chaotic energy that arbitrarily goes everywhere at once. Sporting fans in the emotional rush of a big win behave in chaotic ways, as do game show contestants or anyone whose pent-up frustration and anxiety is suddenly released. This is the manic side of too much wish fulfillment. This extreme feeling never lasts and winds up distorting the way we approach potential opportunities.

In contrast, a Pandora's Box of exaggerated punishment opens whenever we do not get what we want. Here, we are riding a wave of rigidly closed energy that arbitrary deadens our perception. This is the depressive side of too much wish fulfillment. Sporting fans in the emotional rush of a big loss will often behave in a rigidly closed way, experiencing denial, anger and despair. This feeling is akin to a kind of death. We are completely at a loss as to what we most want to do next.

The monumental and arbitrary forces that cause us to feel unnecessarily put upon are largely driven by outcomes that compel us to feel chaotically open or rigidly closed. Especially when no one responds as we do. The systems created by economics, culture and politics are intended to mitigate such exaggerations; however, even at a personal level, it is hard to pull away from the excess of outcome. Compromise can be very hard.

So how does being zanshin change this?

First, by isolating the needs that compel us to behave in extreme ways. Ego protects; Experience discerns; Core Essence confirms. The more we are drawn to use outcomes as a proxy for the need we want to assert, the more we will view the world as arbitrary and capricious. This can be mitigated.

Second, by proposing a Middle Path. When Ego protects, it relies upon unacknowledged defaults. Too much self-promotion causes us to reject the experience of others and forces us to confirm only those outcomes that are important to us. The Middle Path would be to set aside protection and move on to discernment or confirmation. However, that requires restraint and willingness the very qualities get pushed aside when over-protecting.

The zone of optimal decision making is the Middle Path. A decision need not be completely about Ego, Experience or Core Essence. So when we are zanshin, our decisions invite us to be part of something larger than our expectation. We must tolerate an organic sharing that refuses to be constrained by the arbitrary needs of one agency. The tradeoff between risk and reward (when exaggerated by a specific outcome) can push us out of the Zanshin Overlap but only when we use one kind of leverage. The organic nature of the remaining mind never blossoms when we are too attached to outcomes.

When Experience discerns with too much empiricism, it results in disconnection and helplessness; when Core Essence confirms with too much conviction, it leads to a denial of responsibility; and when the Ego protects with too little flexibility, it separates us from the restraint and willingness we otherwise might have. All three cause us to place ourselves above any shared relationship. In contrast, an organically shared relationship offers us the opportunity to be larger than ourselves, by moderating the exaggeration of too much self-promotion. But to get there we must accept the Middle Path. To get there, we must release the logic which each agency uses to narrow our awareness.

Events are sewn into time because we identify them as *temporary* or *permanent* (in duration), as *limited* or *pervasive* (in scope) and as ME or NOT ME (in preference). Because these evaluations are interior to us, we often fail to realize how all three identifications can lead us away from integration and interdependence if we refuse to change our awareness. That's why it is important to find the energy of the Middle Path. We must release the logic which each agency uses.

- If we use a decision to *protect,* Personal Agency dominates; Ego and self-determination will guide us.
- If we use a decision to *discern,* Impersonal Agency dominates; an open-ended evaluation of Experience will guide us.
- If we use a decision to *confirm,* Divine Agency dominates; a trust for how life unfolds will guide us.

The energies that get sewn into time make what we live through identifiable and real to us. They also forecast how we might want to relate to one another with our decisions. The reason we are burdened by the arbitrary is because, amongst ourselves, there is no agreement as to when to best use which approach. Even the most impartial of the three (Impersonal Agency) is problematic because *what* it protects and confirms is still primarily social. The more we evaluate our shared circumstances in exclusionary ways using just one agency, the more anxiety we create. This makes it harder to appreciate the diversity of perspectives which the remaining mind can organize on our behalf.

It all hinges on how we align ourselves with the duration, scope and preference assignments we use. Self-promotion, as a specific way of making a decision, might best be defined as a pattern that generates support and maintenance for our unique way of seeing the world; socially necessary if we want to work cooperatively but also quite risky because it may lead to an exaggerated need for over-protection, over-discernment, and over-confirmation. That's why being zanshin is important.

Suppose our appreciation narrows in a significant and unexpected way (say *duration* changes from temporary to permanent or vice versa in a dramatic way). When that happens, we may find it difficult to express a preference. Looking to others or clinging to an expected outcome may prompt a default response, but that preference will feel tenuous and weak. That shift in perception draws away our energy.

At this point, our decision making may feel both "chaotically open" and "rigidly closed" at the same time. If we are insecure about what we can say *with confidence,* then we may lose the ability to select any agency at all. Developing the patience to work through moments of tension and ambivalence by taking the Middle Path is a necessary prerequisite to being zanshin.

Enslavement by exaggeration only takes away your power. Sensible decisions make light of the arbitrary by forecasting a sustainable and open level of commitment. This is rarely possible without a clearer sense for how our pre-decisions can limit us. This, itself, is a gigantic insight for then we can organically commit to what the remaining mind offers.

To banish the arbitrary, *remember* that time is a continuous medium, so assigning duration, scope and preference must be both a personal choice and an arbitrary one. Time moves relentlessly forward, irrevocably changing the context and carrying *us* along with it, so, of course, we MUST make presumptions about duration, scope, and preference.

Things can be "read" as being *temporary* or *permanent* (in duration), as *limited* or *pervasive* (in scope), and as *useful* or *not* (in preference), so there is no standard, other than the one that we assign. However, once made, *that assignment* becomes *personally* operative. All of our decisions are now "cued" to make that energy (and those assignments) real to us. This is why it is a challenge to be zanshin.

You must give up a small degree of momentary confidence to gain a larger degree of lasting self-direction.

You can do that. Just keep reading!

Interdependence and Integration: The Midpoint of the Pendulum Swing

Alex, the team would be lost without you!

The idea of a "lifeline" option is that a contestant can reduce the arbitrariness of an unknown result by relying upon others. When you rely upon others, you are enhancing your interdependence and integration *with them.* It's not that you don't still have control over your decision, but you are no longer isolated. When you are in the center of the pendulum swing, you are optimizing interdependence and integration by sharing a portion of your decision with those around you. Part of what allows you to accept an unexpected result is the feeling you get from seeing yourself *in others. The zanshin moment is NOT about losing individuality; it is about accepting the place that allows you to be fine exactly the way you are.*

By giving up a small degree of momentary confidence, you gain a larger degree of lasting self-direction. Your acceptance of that idea is what strengthens the shared "lifeline" idea.

Interdependence just works. What we protect, discern and confirm (together) is greater than the small lens we use when making a decision all by ourselves.

We've covered a lot. Let's practice working with these concepts before moving on to what I call "The First Decision."

Comprehension Check

The distinctions I'm raising are hard to grasp without a little practice. Read the following life examples and see how you can flexibly assign duration, scope and preference to individual situations. Remember, there is no "one" answer and there is no "right" answer either.

Life Examples	**Descriptive Associations**
When you were 10 years old, your sister pushed you down the stairs.	Does this feel *temporary* or *permanent* to you? Does this feel *limited* or *pervasive* to you? Are you *drawn to* this or do you want to *distance yourself* from it?
Your boss fired you and you are looking for a new job.	Does this feel *temporary* or *permanent* to you? Does this feel *limited* or *pervasive* to you? Are you *drawn to* this or do you want to *distance yourself* from it?
Your spouse disagrees with your preferences and priorities; she doesn't approve of your child-rearing choices.	Does this feel *temporary* or *permanent* to you? Does this feel *limited* or *pervasive* to you? Are you *drawn to* this or do you want to *distance yourself* from it?
Your father died unexpectedly when you were 8 years old.	Does this feel *temporary* or *permanent* to you? Does this feel *limited* or *pervasive* to you? Are you *drawn to* this or do you want to *distance yourself* from it?
You are jealous of a coworker's success and you are embarrassed by the way you feel.	Does this feel *temporary* or *permanent* to you? Does this feel *limited* or *pervasive* to you? Are you *drawn to* this or do you want to *distance yourself* from it?

The point here is that there is no "one" answer and there is no "right" answer either. The evaluations we make change depending on how we meet the situation. Your decision to understand and see the world *as you do* reflects both a routine evaluation (of the past) and a forward-focused one as well. The future you make depends on the way you construct it. Your past life events are sewn into time and affect your thought process. To be zanshin is to make open-ended assignments and to change them as necessary.

Now let's think about the intensity of these associations. A high intensity association will feel stronger and more persuasive. You will be less likely to alter the way you remember your experience if it holds sufficient intensity. This is not simply a "memory" test; the more you recreate the "experience" of a particular memory, the more that experience will change how you respond to your current environment. Everything that gets sewn into time has some hold over you. You may not be able to immediately lessen that hold, but you can increase your awareness of how all this comes together.

To play with these concepts, fill in the table below. For the life example of "Event," pull out your day planner and select any appointment from last week. Give this event a name and record it below as "Event." For the example of "Place," identify a place where you lived in the past, not your current address. Write down the old place or address. For the example of "Person," select a person whom you know well but do not see regularly. Write down their name below as "Person."

For each identified item, quickly write down some descriptive associations. Think back and identify what you liked or disliked about each (was it pleasurable or painful?). List anything of consequence that was especially relevant to your life or that made a strong and lasting impact on you (if nothing did, then note that as well). Finally, ask yourself: "Five years from now, will I appreciate any of these associations?" If you don't think you'll even remember the item, then list that as well.

Life Examples	Descriptive Associations
Event:	
Place:	
Person:	

The more specific your recollection of the event, place, and person, the more you will be able to identify the various dimensions of your relation. Events, places, and people offer us ways to not only appreciate the world we DID inhabit, but also define the future we WANT to inhabit. The more vivid and intense the association, the more we are unconsciously directed to recreate it through our actions and decisions.

Directions: Referring back to the table you've just completed above, on a scale **from 1 to 5** (with 1 being the lowest intensity and 5 being the highest), how **intense** are your associations with each entry? Remember, there is no "one" answer and there is no "right" answer either.

Life Examples (write in label from the prior table)	Regarding the durability of this experience …	Regarding the scope of this experience …	Regarding the pleasure or pain of this experience …
Event:	Score: __________	Score: __________	Score: __________
Place:	Score: __________	Score: __________	Score: __________
Person:	Score: __________	Score: __________	Score: __________

Lower scores indicate that your associations are **more readily changeable**; higher scores indicate a tendency to see things in ways that make them **harder to overcome**. Strong preferences are part of your historical makeup and personality. The better you know yourself, the better you will be at sizing up the impact a situation might have on your future reactions or responses.

Again, remember that the point here is to see how your decision to understand and see the world ***as you do*** reflects both a routine evaluation (of the past) and a forward-focused one as well. To be zanshin is to make open-ended assignments and to change them as necessary.

In the next exercise, you will look at facts and conventions that you might typically encounter on any given day. When someone misattributes or misapplies those facts and conventions, we often feel a strong need to correct the situation in some way. Part of our need to correct is a wish to maintain *our* perspective on a situation. These "judgements" are often personalized; however, they do not need to be. Please identify the duration, scope, and preference response you associated with each of the following. Don't overthink your answers; it's more fun if you don't.

Facts and Conventions	If the situation, as described, were continued ...
You were out at a shopping mall, and you saw a man trying to walk backwards down an escalator moving in the opposite direction.	What do you most want to do? ________________ Does the violated convention feel *temporary* or *permanent* to you? ________________ Does the disruption feel *limited* or *pervasive* to you? ________________ Are you *drawn to* this or do you want to *distance yourself* from it?
You are out in public and you watch a little boy blow his nose on someone else's sleeve, who doesn't seem to notice.	What do you most want to do? ________________ Does the violated convention feel *temporary* or *permanent* to you? ________________ Does the disruption feel *limited* or *pervasive* to you? ________________ Are you *drawn to* this or do you want to *distance yourself* from it?

Facts and Conventions	If the situation, as described, were continued ...
A man comes into a store and proceeds to pay for everything he buys using only pennies, which take a long time to count.	What do you most want to do? __________ Does the violated convention feel *temporary* or *permanent* to you? __________ Does the disruption feel *limited* or *pervasive* to you? __________ Are you *drawn to* this or do you want to *distance yourself* from it?
A family enters a store and all of the family members are wearing large, square block shoes which you have never seen before.	What do you most want to do? __________ Does the violated convention feel *temporary* or *permanent* to you? __________ Does the disruption feel *limited* or *pervasive* to you? __________ Are you *drawn to* this or do you want to *distance yourself* from it?

Facts and Conventions	If the situation, as described, were continued ...
You listen to a person rationalize that the end of the world is near, then he asks you if he can buy an insurance policy to cover that.	What do you most want to do? __________ Does the violated convention feel *temporary* or *permanent* to you? __________ Does the disruption feel *limited* or *pervasive* to you? __________ Are you *drawn to* this or do you want to *distance yourself* from it?

The point here is that the more dissonance that is created through the attitudes, actions and behaviors we anticipate and expect *from others,* the more we are forced to acknowledge that we have attitudes, judgements and opinions that are constructed by virtue of remembered experience. The duration, scope, and preference we associate with that experience are primarily habits of convention. The more we reinforce them, the harder they are to change. We are much more interdependently aware than we care to admit. Every time we try to correct the behavior of others, we are trying to enforce a certain standard that may or may not apply to them. Greater awareness of yourself and how you operate is the beginning of becoming zanshin.

Remember the three examples that I showed you: (1) Incomplete information, (2) Lack of priority, and (3) Conflict with the past? What you need to do in each case is be clearer about *the commitment that you are creating with yourself.* Duration, scope and preference are malleable associations. The question is where do you want to be on the pendulum swing and what might you have to give up if you want to stay there? It might take a little while to let go of what we thought was "right," but your choice to become zanshin will guide you.

I'll have more to say about these three examples later.

Conclusion

Decision making can be viewed as a Utility Pendulum. We make decisions so that we can self-identify with our choices. It will always be easier to base our decisions from the ME | NOT ME extremes since we know that we have the authority to use those perspectives. But you can be more.

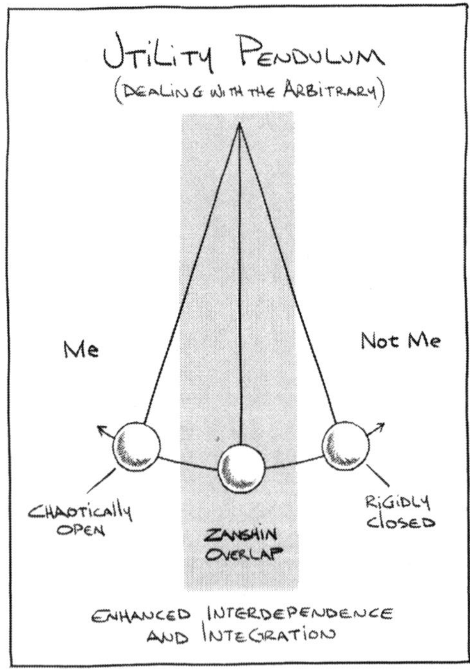

What is the power that is inside your decisions? That power comes from choosing to be zanshin. The more you can move to the center of the pendulum swing, the more effective and flexible your decision making will be and the more you will embrace growth and change. Feeling open, uncommitted and relaxed is an ideal way to be. That can be yours.

CHAPTER 2:

The First Decision: Dealing with the Arbitrary

CHAPTER 2:
The First Decision

Plato's allegory of the charioteer (reason) harnessed to two horses (appetite and spirit) makes the point that what drives us forward is appetite and spirit. If reason is presumed to be separate from those drivers, then the resulting logic (or the conveyance for reason) can become wooden and lifeless. Reason orients and harnesses our passions, but it cannot be separate from them. So to move in the direction of the worthy, truthful and virtuous (the qualities which Reinhold Niebuhr celebrates), our decisions must participate with reason, appetite and spirit but in ways that are larger than organized logic. As Niebuhr said, *"Nothing worth doing is completed in our lifetime; therefore we must be saved by hope."* The more our decisions move in the direction of the worthy, truthful and virtuous, the more enlarged they will be, not by logic, but by something altogether different—the Zanshin Overlap and the remaining mind.

This chapter introduces the First Decision. To make that decision, the charioteer must drive *without his chariot.* Hard to imagine, but this is essential if we going to use the energies found in the remaining mind.

The Arbitrariness of Pressure

Some days, I can't even get around to procrastinating.

With pressure to "discern" and "confirm" what others want, we often feel we don't have what it takes. We procrastinate to protect ourselves. "Do it now!" is the vulnerability we generate once we assume that the wooden chariot (and its logic) cannot be taken away. Our fears point to the arbitrariness of what is being "given" to us.

Our first decision must answer the question: how shall we deal with the arbitrary? Certainly there is no lifetime project that holds greater intensity than feeling arbitrarily "put upon" by others. We must cultivate hope, faith and love—otherwise we become blind to what we do share and mute to the promise we might share together.

Duration, Scope and Preference

I consider myself a passionate man, but of course, a lawyer first.

As the son of a lawyer, "lawyerly" passions ran high in my family, and of course, with the law, you must put your trust in legal concepts. That brings me back to duration, scope and preference. While these are not legal concepts, they do have "lawyerly" limitations; we often feel bound to them as fixed ideas, even though there is an arbitrary quality to how they work either *for* us or *against* us.

You may have been surprised with the comprehension check exercises at the close of the previous chapter. I hope so. It is much easier to test the veracity of what we are doing with duration, scope and preference assignments once these concepts are understandable and clear.

Now, let's try a thought experiment.

Evaluate the following investment scenarios and decide which investment option you want to go with. Financial decisions are unlike other decisions because they are future-focused "speculations" and, as they say, "past performance is not indicative of future results." There is no guaranteed reference point to guide you.

With speculative decisions, we don't know how to make a credible assignment with regard to *risk* or *opportunity.* That makes it much easier to see what is really going on with the fixed ideas that come to us as duration, scope and preference.

Ready? You have the option to invest in one of the following. Which one will you choose?

Option 1:
A 5-year Treasury bond that pays 2.5% compounding annually. You will receive your principle and interest back at the end of the 5-year term. The $50,000 investment that you make today will grow to $56,570. Over five years, you will earn $6,570—guaranteed by contract.

Option 2:
A Standard & Poor's Index investment that has an average annual return over the last five years of 10.91%. The actual annual rate over the last five years varied from a low of 1.38% to a high of 32.39%. Over the last 10 years, the annual return was negative only once (2008). The $50,000 investment that you make today will grow to an unknown amount and it may lose value.

Option 3:
A $50,000 investment in a kitchen renovation. The return on this investment is unknown; however, the lifetime enjoyment is expected to be high. Kitchen renovations in your area are "paying back" 85% of the initial investment; however, the overall market is appreciating on average 4% per year, so that $50,000 should be completely recovered by the fifth year. There is, however, no guarantee, and you might lose money.

Since all future returns have absolutely nothing to do with you personally, they are, in essence, arbitrary and, for the moment, completely unknown (except that 5-year Treasury bond). The only reason you have fixed ideas about these options is because of the possible risk or opportunity they hold for you, and because you must decide. (Here, the wooden planks of logic serve as a sort of terra firma. You are depending on them to convey you from point A to point B, even though you do not know the final outcome.)

So, how will you evaluate the risk and the opportunity? Will it be based on an anticipated outcome? Or based on a relationship that you cultivate around risk and opportunity?

Let's review duration, scope and preference.

Duration (or **Durability**)—How long might this event last—is it permanent or temporary?

Five years is the stated duration; however, what is at stake is the durability of your current feeling. If you pick the right investment, the good feeling of your current condition will continue. If you pick wrong, that good feeling may turn against you. The $50,000 that you put into this investment is simply a reflection of that. Are you going to be fearful or hopeful? Can you be "durably" happy if the investment does not turn out as you expect?

- **Risk:** A potential loss in current good feeling.
- **Opportunity:** A potential increase in that good feeling.

Scope (or **Importance**)—How pervasive is this event—is its importance "universal" or is the importance particular and specific?

The anticipated rates of return are the primary indicators of scope. Which is more important to you?

- A guaranteed $6,570 improvement,
- A potential 10.91% improvement—with no guarantee, or
- A lifestyle improvement that may or may not pay back in five years.

While these returns may seem very particular and specific, with your scope evaluation, you are also trying to decide upon their more "universal" importance. What does this decision say about you and who you are? The fact that you can get any of these potential returns can make you feel good about your place in the world. The fact that any of one of these might not go as you expect can make you feel lousy in a very personal way. The $50,000 that you put into this investment is now a reflection of your own competence. Can you be universally happy with who you are if the impact does not turn out the way you expect?

- **Risk:** A potential loss in personal self-image.
- **Opportunity:** A potential increase in personal self-image.

Preference (or **Preferential Feeling**)—Does this seem like a ME event or a NOT ME event? Are you drawn to it and want it to last longer and be part of you? Or do you want to dismiss it and throw it away as quickly as possible?

Your preference is largely a *triggered* response. You are automatically drawn into a potential option or thrown out of it.

One way to understand this response is through what psychologists call "temporal discounting." If a future benefit is too distant in time, it may cease to feel valuable. Psychologists tell us that people discount an anticipated future benefit by as much as half. That means we overemphasize the status quo and assume it will continue, even if we have the potential to change it. Risk and opportunity are relative to the current moment.

Another way to look at this preferential feeling is in the way we give ourselves "full credit and full license" to decide as we want. "Full credit and full license" is an interesting phrase. If you are given "full credit" to make whatever decision you want, then the credit which accrues as a result of your decision—that is, its benefit or advantage—is yours. You are synonymous with your decision. Likewise, if you are given "full license" to make whatever decision you want, then no one stands in your way. Interdependence is no longer a factor. You are, in theory, independent of the larger social environment. The ME | NOT ME utility you align with when you are given full credit and full license, becomes the driving force that allows you to set aside all the troubling and contradictory aspects of shared interdependence.

Preferential feeling is a kind of litmus test. Is the anticipated future attractive enough to set aside the status quo and do we give ourselves full credit and full license to decide as we want? When the opportunity (or the risk) seems great enough, we act. When it does not, we stay put; we remain indecisive.

The $50,000 and the potential returns that we might get are now being organized based on the power that we give ourselves. How do we see the future and are we confident enough to make a decision?

- **Risk:** A potential loss in a future that *disconfirms* your understanding of the world and erodes your confidence.
- **Opportunity:** A confirmation in your ability to organize the future that you want expands your confidence.

Did you notice how self-referential these are? Duration is about the *current good feeling*; scope is about our *personal self-image;* and preferential feeling is about our *general level of confidence.* Here are the wooden planks that logic uses to convey meaning and power to what we decide.

Let's go back and look at some of the Comprehension Check examples.

Life Examples	Descriptive Associations
When you were ten years old, your sister pushed you down the stairs.	Does this feel *temporary* or *permanent* to you? **If your current good feeling is high, this will seem temporary; if your current good feeling is damaged by that memory, this will seem permanent.** Does this feel *limited* or *pervasive* to you? **If your current self-image is high, this will seem limited; if your current self-image is damaged by that memory, this will seem pervasive.** Are you *drawn to* this or do you want to *distance yourself* from it? **If your confidence level is high, you will distance yourself from it; if your confidence level is low, you will be drawn into it. The memory, in its way, needs to be fixed. Until you make amends, grieve a loss or forgive a trespass, your confidence may be negatively impacted.**

From your own life examples, pick the event, place, or person that received your *highest score* for intensity:

Life Examples	Descriptive Associations
Event, Place or Person:	Does this recollection impact you: By increasing or decreasing your current good feeling? YES | NO By increasing or decreasing your self-image? YES | NO By increasing or decreasing your confidence level? YES | NO

The more intensely you feel an event, place or person, the more any increase or decrease will be noticed. I'm betting that for the one life example with the highest score, you will feel a strong YES to each of the questions.

Consider how you answered the following example from the Fact and Convention table:

Facts and Conventions	If the situation, as described, were to continue ...
You listen to a person rationalize that the end of the world is near, then he asks you if he can buy an insurance policy to cover that.	What do you most want to do here? **Laugh and walk away.** Does the violated convention feel *temporary* or *permanent* to you? **Temporary, this is about the other person, not you (your current level of good feeling is not changed).** Does the disruption that results feel *limited* or *pervasive* to you? **Limited, you can walk away (because this does not impact your self-image—if it did impact your self-image, you might want to punch him out).** Are you *drawn to* this or do you want to *distance yourself* from it? **Distance yourself (you remain confident in your ability to organize your future).**

The reason why indecision can be such a problem is that the reason, appetite and spirit *inform* logic; but logic cannot *constrain* them. Risk and opportunity spring out of our pre-decisions, yet we must always be ready to change those pre-decisions.

To be zanshin is to realize that the relationship you have will always be *with yourself* and to know that the remaining mind will always, yes *always,* include others and the world at large.

To test that idea, go back to the ME feelings that were listed earlier (safety, peace, respect, belonging, etc.). Ask yourself: When you feel favorably treated by others, how likely is it that all of the preferential feelings will be true for you in a positive way?

Answer: You will feel safety, peace, respect, and belonging. The next moment will be informed but not constrained by what you realize. Shifting freely is possible.

Now look at the NOT ME feelings (afraid, angry, disrespected, excluded, etc.). Ask yourself: When you feel UN-favorably treated by others, how likely is it that all of the preferential feelings will be true for you in a negative way?

Answer: You will feel afraid, angry, disrespected, and excluded. Here again, the next moment is informed but not constrained by what you realize. Negativity is changeable.

That said, we are sensitive to what accompanies these triggers. Good feeling arrives with a sense of hope. A vibrant self-image can produce an outlook of faith, and a high level of confidence enables us to do our best. But the more wooden these become by the arbitrariness of personality and convention, the more inflexible our evaluations will be.

Because we are more inclined to remember negative events rather than positive ones, we struggle to make decisions that we can live with. The more our decisions move in the direction of the worthy, truthful and virtuous, the more they will be enlarged by faith, hope and love. If we let go of the tight grip of outcomes that logic uses to protect, discern and confirm our separateness, then we are becoming more be zanshin.

Appreciating the Arbitrary

I think I'll take the murder.

The dynamic inside every decision is a simple one: Turn an arbitrary NOT ME event about the past into a more acceptable ME event about the future. This tug of war is not just a test of will, stamina and power; it is often a reasoned test of logic around the integrity of interests. Turning the NOT ME into ME is the epic battle we face every day to alter the future so it comports not with the past, but with the logic of personality and convention. The prevalence of an arbitrary decision (and its presumed utility) indicates how willingly we fall asleep.

If you pick up a newspaper or listen to the news, you hear stories all the time that employ a simple strategy—make the two sides appear equally arbitrary in what they are seeking. Take for example, the California high school teacher who sued the labor union because he believed it should be his choice to support a union and its causes. He made the remark that he got to choose what movie he attended, what church he went to, what gym he went to, and he should have the same right to choose to support a union or not. He felt he was being forced to pay to support positions that he didn't agree with. He sued the union, stating a violation of his First Amendment rights.

The situational tension required to turn a NOT ME event into a ME event is the stuff of legendary comedy. Imagine clowns tripping over their too big shoes trying to carry the weight of human happenstance as they struggle to overcome the monumental and arbitrary forces bent on continuously trying to push them down.

Let me paint a visual for you. Imagine Charlie Chaplin as the "Tramp," entering the Supreme Court as the justices argue the constitutionality of mandatory union payments. The Tramp rises from his chair in his black cut-away jacket and bowler hat with fists waving in the air while he crosses to one especially surly justice and exclaims, "*I get to choose* what movie I want to go see."

The justice scowls, prompting a quick about-face. Chaplin exclaims even louder, "*I get to choose* what church I want to go to." Then he falls kneeling on the ground, mimicking whimpering a prayer that he knows is futile. He continues, "*I get to choose* what gym I want to join." While on his knees, he mimics lifting a 500-pound weight, which he attempts to throw at the justices.

Rising back to his feet, he mounts a chair and he says, "*Why shouldn't I decide* if I want to support a union?" Then suddenly the seat of his chair falls away and he ignominiously falls through. As the scene ends, Chaplin looks as if he is sitting chest high in a toilet bowl!

Whichever side of the argument the clown represents really doesn't much matter. The same scene could be rendered just as effectively with Chaplin taking on the role of a Supreme Court justice fed up with the antics of union plaintiffs. In this case, the final tableau would be virtually the same. After standing on a more regal throne as a Supreme Court justice, the breakaway bottom would fall out and the message would be exactly the same: despite our best efforts, occasionally, even a Supreme Court justice feels like he, too, is sitting chest high in a toilet bowl.

The comic depiction of such a human struggle endures as a necessary metaphor because the problem of being treated arbitrarily is so universal. Turning an arbitrary NOT ME event about the past into a more acceptable ME event about the future is a connecting point that all of us share, and more often than not, we cannot see past the preoccupying divisions that focus our energies.

A clown's artistry is his ability to reflect back the pain we hold in secret because, in the logic of the arbitrary, we cannot expect others to be there for us, *so why show them* what they will ridicule anyway? We preserve our sense of dignity by holding in secret both our pain *and* our joy. The dynamic the clown illustrates is that "winning" the battle to overcome the arbitrary is hopelessly conflicted because the problem never goes away. The satisfaction, happiness, and joy that we momentarily gain is often at the expense of others, so rather than openly proclaim the satisfaction we achieve, we try to minimize it and hide it. Too much demonstration of either pain or joy can weaken the balance of our dependence on others. Even in our satisfaction, we are sad for others; and even in our sadness, we can be happy for them as well. The dilemma is always about our interdependence and how it impacts us in contradictory ways.

To be zanshin is to bring forward and lift up all of these contradictory angles. The love-loss | pleasure-pain dynamic that we build into our choices and decisions is made all the more complex (and beautiful) because the balance of our dependence can be so utterly contradictory. Like the seesaw in the park, the upside and downside are moving to create a shared experience, so it is not really about who is "up" and who is "down." Any evaluation of outcome misses the point. We are in a relation that is greater than any one outcome.

By comprehending that, we start to see how *really hard* it is to be interdependent. To be zanshin requires a willing interdependence that we must create inside ourselves.

Every clown wants what he wants, and every clown is willing—sometimes very willing—to deal arbitrarily with others. That's why we fear clowns. We are reminded that the world doesn't necessarily respond to what we want. Clowns may be funny, but they are also just a tiny bit frightening.

It's hard to be zanshin and to rise above the clown's antics without first appreciating what we do to ourselves. It's not that our thoughts and decisions are "wrong" or even "wrong-headed"—just *incomplete.* We must be gentle, forgiving and understanding before we move to fulfill our preference with self-aggrandizing force.

That is, after all, what we laugh at most, the clown who really doesn't know what he is doing. He struggles to maintain the good feeling, personal self-image, and level of confidence he has (just like we do). The more the world decides to beat up on *him,* the happier we become. "*He* must not understand the world very well," we tell ourselves, and in between our bouts of laughter, we are thanking our lucky stars that it's him and not us.

> **Zanshin Observation:** Good feeling is about us, individually; self-image is about sharing ourselves with others; and confidence is about the unfolding nature of what happens. When you are zanshin, you negotiate all three while giving only one your direct attention.

Economics versus Object Relations

George is getting into object relations – he's not taking any chances.

Duration, scope and preference help us "see" the world. They reflect back our clown-like need to make the world into something we can relate to. Like George here, we cannot know with certainty how things will turn out, so if we are not zanshin, we will make decisions based on the outcomes that support our biased blind spots. (As we shall see, the bias blind spot is the classic cognitive bias that reconfirms the way we already see the world.)

Protection (like much of confirmation) is a persistent wish to maintain outcomes that resist growth and change. As we shall see with Divine Agency, when growth and change *expand* what is possible, our good feeling, self-image and confidence will change right along with it. That which is worthy, truthful and virtuous is *already* assured, provided our biased blind spots do not conflict.

But I'm getting ahead of myself.

Economics is the study of outcomes. Choices are made to create specific outcomes; we organize these outcomes to maximize fulfillment. Duration, scope and preference reconfirm the good feeling, self-image and level of confidence that best expresses our need for fulfillment—even when that fulfillment turns out to be somewhat clown-like.

What we often do not realize is how imprecisely determined risk and opportunity genuinely are. "The gut rules the measure"[4] because duration, scope and preference are evaluations that remake the world into something we recognize and understand.

With too much emphasis on outcomes, the question becomes: what happens when the logic each agency uses actually narrows our awareness *too much*? Pre-decisions can conflict. If the "gut rules the measure" and tells one group to protect, then those who wish to discern or confirm (rather than protect) are going to feel left out. Too narrow a focus on one need pushes out others.

---

4 "The gut rules the measure" is a quotation from Peter Bernstein, *Against the Gods: The Remarkable Story of Risk.* It implies that future forecasting cannot be quantified.

Too much demand around one need prompts a zero-sum game; that is, a self-defeating loss of *inter*dependence.

Economics is the science of decision making because it illustrates our need for forward-focused action. Resource allocation, planning and goal setting all have economic underpinnings. We must understand and accept the zero-sum equation of "if this" then "not that." Things cannot be in two places at the same time.

So, from an economics point of view, we put a lot of energy into evaluating outcomes. The problem is that every attempt to achieve an outcome puts pressure on the way we support one another. In the logic of the arbitrary, we cannot expect others to be there for us, so why show them what they will ridicule anyway? We preserve our sense of dignity by holding, in secret, our pain *or* our joy. The more we focus on outcomes, the less cooperative we become so even when we *do* agree, we are unwilling to show any emotion lest it be turned against us. The wooden planks of logic make all forms of sharing harder to achieve when the needs that they serve are treated differently. Personal Agency, Impersonal Agency and Divine Agency make different evaluations. Each views the other as misaligned or off-target.

In contrast, let's compare economics to object relations, which analyzes how relational patterns change so they can create enhanced interdependence and integration. The more we perceive our relation in a fixed way, the more that relation will be seen in an arbitrary way, which eventually does open the door for integration because our evaluations are more fluid than we assume. Nothing remains fixed and everything is open to integration provided we are given the support of interdependence and the life lines that we extend to one another.

Object relations studies the swing in our relational patterns (from ME to NOT ME) and how they shift over time. The natural resting point for a relationship (in object relations theory) is in the center of the pendulum swing. The world is not exclusively ME or NOT ME. The complex world of cooperation is the in-between world—somewhere between the excesses of the two extremes. The zero-sum of "if this" then "not that" need not be the only way to organize our efforts. We do not have to hold in secret our pain and joy if we can choose to accommodate one another with openness and trust. If the gut rules the measure, then the challenge of the biased blind spot is how it reconfirms our way of understanding the world, even though the biased blind spot makes interdependence significantly harder to achieve.

Object relations is about integrating opposites and becoming more zanshin. It's about learning to overcome the biased blind spot. If we tolerate ambiguity and trust ourselves, then the tension of unknown outcomes cannot defeat us. Like any combination of opposites, the pattern—thesis, antithesis and synthesis—offers unexpected results. Risk and opportunity are not as fixed as we assume.

Like a tightrope walker, the two sides support us, but only if we are zanshin enough to trust the remaining mind. The center will hold, but we cannot put all of our attention on outcomes.

Too much concentration on outcomes and we lose power. Challenging decisions DO upset the good feeling, self-image, and level of confidence that we (and others) want. However, to be zanshin is to know that your power comes from the relationship you have with yourself *and with* the remaining mind—not from an outcome or how that outcome may be enhanced or made more difficult by others.

The opposing sides, the "Go! Go! Go!" or the "Fall! Fall! Fall!," *can be* resolved by trusting the place in between. This is the Zanshin Overlap. The remaining mind gives us the courage that otherwise we would not feel as real or as available if we were unable to integrate the opposing extremes. The zanshin remaining mind is not (or more strongly cannot) be limited by the unreconciled logic of either side.

Object Relations and the Good Breast-Bad Breast

The breast that feeds the hungry infant is the "good breast," while a hungry infant that finds no breast is in relation to the "bad breast.[5]" Good Breast-Bad Breast is one of the more famous phrases in object relations. The explanatory phrase "in relation to," is pivotal because the baby will have no response without some experienced relation that means something. What the infant experiences as good or bad is constantly being held up for mental review, especially when there are sharp divisions. The good breast of "fulfillment" and the bad breast of "nothing" (or loss of fulfillment) are eventually integrated into a whole that is neither good nor bad. Ambiguity is eventually tolerated and transformed into a complex picture that does not easily gravitate to any one "frame" or characterization.

What we sew into time is both a feeling and a thinking awareness. The duration, scope and preference which qualify our opinions and judgements are constantly held up for mental review. That which is felt at one time and place is compared to that which is felt at a different time and place. Over time we get pulled along by the energy of our preferences, which, in turn, begins to shape the duration and scope we assign incrementally to each new event. These partial experiences (or mentally-constructed "part objects") are integrated into more comprehensive whole objects. This integration corresponds with our ability to tolerate ambiguity, to see how both the "good" and the "bad" breast are a part of the same mother figure. Fortunately,

5 Good Breast-Bad Breast theory originated with Mélanie Klein (1952); later popularized by Fairbairn, W. R. D., *An Object-Relations Theory of the Personality.* New York: Basic Books, (1952).

these associations are constantly updated and revised. So while "There is nothing either good or bad, but thinking makes it so," the standard that "reifies" our preferred way of seeing the world is located primarily *within us* and within the relations that are most important to us.

Zanshin Observation: To pre-decide invites our attention, but to protect, discern and confirm clarifies exactly how and why we are being triggered.

The first decision is the most instrumental: How will we deal with the arbitrary? Where do we go to get some rest from its pressures and burdens?

- Will we deal with the arbitrary by rationalizing our situation through a model of interpretation that causes us to feel and/or think in specific ways?

- Or will we include ourselves in the very next moment because we can deal with the arbitrary in an inclusive way?

The first alternative increases our awareness for obstacles, pressures and fears. The second increases our awareness of what supports us on either side of a decision. Interestingly, the second alternative also increases what Daniel J. Siegel, in his book, *Mindsight*, labels "SAFE" behavior (Stable, Adaptive, Flexible, and Energized).[6]

Don't you want to feel SAFE? Don't you want to expand your understanding of the ME | NOT ME tug of war so your good feeling, self-image and confidence are less threatened?

By focusing on a relational model rather than an economic one, we are given the freedom to look past the narrow limits we construct by pre-deciding a response based on an outcome. The more we let our pre-decisions illustrate the aspirations of faith, hope and love, the more humane and caring our decisions will become.

To some, this line of reasoning may appear entirely backwards. To give preferential priority to one's hope rather than to a specific outcome is to prioritize a fiction rather than a reality. Intuitively, one might argue that relationships *are limited.* That is exactly what it means to be an adult and to use reason and not passion. Reality does not bend to the whim of relation. To this critique, I point out that any model of interpretation that requires us to think and feel in specific ways is, in some way, limited. The first decision *is* the most instrumental: How do you want to deal with the arbitrary? To rationalize every decision on the basis of obstacles and outcomes serves only to heighten the arbitrary nature of conflict and our inability to draw a more connective awareness from what we decide together—a connective awareness that with confidence and trust will *increase* one's feeling of expansion. This is the benefit of interdependence, the willing inclusion of others that expands what is available for all.

---

6 Siegel, *Mindsight: The New Science of Personal Transformation*, Bantam Books, 2010, p. 70.

To deepen our understanding of inclusion and why it can feel threatening, we must look at reason, logic, appetite and spirit and how they coordinate with duration, scope and preference. The First Decision often boils down to personality. So let's start there.

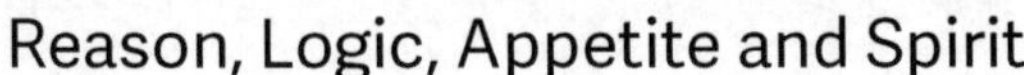

Reason, Logic, Appetite and Spirit

Not on your life!!!

Everyone wants to speed along. Yet, conspiracy theorists are prone to see "if-then" scenarios that make life more threatening than necessary. "Not on your life!" envisages a conspiracy that simply magnifies the arbitrary. Talk about personality.

Reason, logic, appetite and spirit are the unique parts associated with personality. When combined together they help you make decisions. Your personality need not magnify the arbitrary; it can reduce the arbitrary. However, you cannot use personality to double-down on the logic that automatically justifies your pre-decisions.

Plato allegorized the decision-maker to help us explain why we have trouble with decisions. Here are my definitions for what was illustrated at the start of this chapter:

- **Reason** creates your awareness for time and its impact. As events are sewn into time, you identify them as being *temporary* or *permanent* (in duration) and you acknowledge time's relentless and irreversible impacts as being *pervasive* or *limited* (in scope), and *useful* or *not* (in preference). The preferential feeling, which reason reinforces, leads to the love-loss | pleasure-pain dynamic that is naturally part of your decisions. With reason, you balance out the conflicting signals that appetite and spirit create.
- **Logic** is what you do with your future awareness. It involves planning and prioritizing your decisions, which would be difficult without a consistent "pattern." Logic is learned and often unrecognized because it is built into our biased blind spot. With logic, you rationalize the pre-decision that triggers your attention. You always have the choice to sew into time a different reason and a different logic; however, *that* takes a lot of self-awareness.
- **Appetite** and **Spirit** include the natural, human faculties you have been given.
    - **Appetite** is worldly desire for experience and connection; appetite is concrete and repetitive.
    - **Spirit** is the perennial desire for change and transformation via freedom and free will; spirit is highly individual, enabling us to live in very unique ways.

If these definitions feel complex, remember that cartoon of the unyielding driver. Reason, logic, appetite and spirit are aspects of personality. The wooden planks that make conspiracy theories possible use the logic working through our pre-decisions. The more we depend on the conveyance of this type of logic, the more limited we become.

When your decision-making approach (or stance) makes use of reason, logic, appetite and spirit, your personality combines them to protect your understanding of the world. Conspiracy theories are not arbitrary, they are illustrations of how we choosing to see the world. This, in turn, illustrates the centering power of Personal Agency.

"Not on your life" is both a rallying cry and a threat. We do become charged up when our will is squashed. So it is no surprise that we actually enjoy this kind of excess.

If the unyielding driver could move to a more impersonal stance (one that could put aside his understanding of the world), that would illustrate Impersonal Agency. Any open-ended decision that discerns (in an unbiased way) an alternative explanation would offer that driver more options than he has right now. However to achieve that, the driver's personality would, accordingly, have to shift.

Alternatively, when our decision-making stance shifts to Divine Agency, we are no longer trying to experience our understanding of the world nor are we trying to discern an unbiased explanation. Here, we are concerned simply with a wish to lighten the impact of the experience that makes the conspiracy theory real to us. It's about turning a "burden" into a "blessing," about trusting ourselves, and about valuing an alternative way of life that we have not tried before. This, too, would signal a shift in that driver's personality.

The conspiracy we have is that our perceptions MUST BE RIGHT. If we protect too much, discern too hard or force a confirmation, then the conspiracy theory that combines with our bias blind spot may need the reality check that only Divine Agency can offer. What breaks open then is larger than anything we might have expected. With Divine Agency we enact a free fall to a new place, because even our personalities *can* be malleable. To shake off the hidden limitations we carry we must tap into new personality reserves.

That's why being zanshin can be so useful.

But to get there, we must first be Stable, Adaptive, Flexible, and Energized (SAFE). We cannot be that unyielding driver. All three agencies and the "differing personalities" they require are more useful when accessed from the midpoint of the pendulum swing. Only there can we find the stillness that speaks more definitively to us than what we, ourselves, can create.

Agency	Personal Agency	Impersonal Agency	Divine Agency
What it does	Builds upon duration, scope and preference	Sets aside duration, scope and preference	Transforms duration, scope and preference
What it does when most active	Explains, rationalizes and justifies our way of seeing based on our good feeling, self-image and level of confidence	Uncovers the relationship we are having without referring to the good feeling, self-image and level of confidence we have	Transforms the relationship we are having by changing the way we hold onto the good feeling, self-image and level of confidence in our relationships
How it does it	Places our attention on the presumptions we make so we can organize a direction for our actions that is consistent with those actions	Suspends our default presumption by having us uncover new and previously undiscovered information	Resets our default presumption by enacting a free fall to a new place, which turns a "burden" into a "blessing"

Illustrating the First Decision

The first decision is the most instrumental:

- Will you deal with the arbitrary by rationalizing your situation through a model of interpretation that causes you to feel and/or think in specific ways?
- Or will you include yourself in the very next moment because you can deal with the arbitrary in an inclusive way?

Below are two profiles. As decision makers, each person must decide how they want to approach their situation. The four parts of personality are illustrated to help you identify the "personality" tradeoffs which the first decision may require.

Type-A Walter. Walter has a Type A personality: competitive, outgoing, ambitious, impatient and aggressive. He runs his office like a personal kingdom; however, Walter's problem is *anger.* He does not accept frustration easily.

Walter is currently negotiating with a supplier over the delay of a production part. The contract spelled out terms: the supplier could offer two alternative delivery dates. To Walter, the later date is unacceptable.

Let's step through the four parts of personality to see how Walter is "making sense" of his situation.

- Walter's guiding reason is equal to his good feeling, self-image and confidence. Any delay would be a permanent future problem, as there is a whole chain of events that would have to be adjusted. The delay would cause a pervasive systemwide obstacle; either the company would have to accept the delay or find another supplier. Walter does not believe this can be done. Walter's clear preference is to make sense of the situation by making the supplier "the undisciplined child who needs to be disciplined."
- The logic that Walter builds upon is anything that makes his reasoning "reasonable" to him: *(1) System constraints.* Walter identified several constraints in the manufacturing process that made the later alternative date impossible; *(2) Information constraints.* Walter identified a lack of information. The time is too short to find a new supplier; and *(3) Marketing constraints.* Walter identified the upcoming sales contracts that would be in jeopardy because of the alternative date.
- The appetite that is feeding Walter's pre-decision coordinates and reinforces his assessment of the duration, scope, and

preference: Walter is on track to be the company's next CEO. If he is able to show three more quarters of stellar results, it is likely that he will earn himself the top spot.

- The spirit that is opposing Walter's pre-decision is unique to Walter. Walter values effectiveness, but he also values a light-hearted sympathy that allows people to be present—not just focusing on results, outcomes, and consequences. The more he persistently ignores his desire for light-hearted sympathy, the more Walter is wearing down his energy by generating anger and frustration.

To resolve the conflict between appetite and spirit, Walter must give greater energy to what the spirit can offer by optimistically orienting himself towards *that*, rather than towards the risks and rewards that he is putting at the forefront of his awareness. Anger is not his natural priority. To gain more from his position as a future CEO, Walter must tolerate ambiguity without becoming personally invested in outcomes he cannot control.

- If Walter rationalizes his situation through a model of interpretation that causes him to feel and/or think in specific ways, he will protect his more limited way of understanding his situation.
- If Walter includes himself in the very next moment after his decision, he will see how mutuality and trust are earned by both sides. To protect, discern and confirm *that,* Walter will need greater flexibility and openness.

After several rounds of compromise, Walter accepted the later delivery date. By openly considering his options, a compromise in the manufacturing process was instituted. Future contracts would specify an even earlier ship date, allowing for more lag time. Walter's attention to both sides of the issue earned him the reputation he needed to become CEO. He still struggles with instantaneous anger and frustration, but accommodating others is slowly becoming easier.

Social-Influencing Amy. Amy is charming, popular, inspiring, emotional and generous. She runs her office with an open-door emphasis and is always engaged in "instrumental" conversations. Amy's problem, however, is *resentment.* She does not accept other people's distrust easily.

In negotiating terms with a new client on an advertising campaign, Amy was trying to arrange a large meeting with all of the various stakeholders so she could pitch the vision and process she wanted to implement. The client (a vice president) was limiting her access to some of the most important people, citing what seemed, to Amy, to be minor constraints: location and schedule. Nothing she proposed seemed to dissuade the VP's concerns.

Let's step through the four parts of personality to see how Amy is "making sense" of her situation.

- Amy's guiding pre-decision is that without the correct input now, she will have a permanent future problem—the implementation process might be focused on the wrong goals and the stakeholders involved might sabotage the campaign. That would create clear and pervasive obstacle; she might have to devote a lot of energy to gathering information and never reach a clear consensus. Amy was doubtful this could be done at a later date. Amy's clear preference was to read into the VP's attitude a lack of trust and an inability to appreciate and value Amy's perspective on the situation. Amy's good feeling, self-image and confidence are all potentially threatened by this situation.
- Amy's logic builds on past experience, which Amy's reasoning defined as "reasonable" to her. *(1) Necessity requires this meeting.* Amy identified several constraints that might harm the value of the campaign if the inputs were offered later. *(2) Location and schedule are minor, not major constraints.* Amy identified this distortion as proof of a poor attitude. *(3) Future coordination will be twice as hard.* To Amy, the

inability to arrive at a viable location and schedule was proof that coordination would be a continuous problem and that, potentially, unstated anger and distrust would make the situation more difficult.

- The appetite that is feeding Amy's pre-decision reinforces her assessment: Amy's most recent client did not offer the necessary inputs in a timely fashion. If Amy wants to show her boss some improvement, then this needs to be handled without his input.
- The spirit that is opposing Amy's unconscious pre-decision is unique to Amy. Resentment is creating a spiritual problem. She values her ability to influence others and when she cannot, she turns that into a referendum on her own sense of worth. Amy's insecurity is driven by context; when work is the primary concern, every client has the potential to make her "look bad." The more Amy persistently ignores her desire for unconditional self-worth, the more she is wearing down her energy by generating resentment.

To resolve the conflict between appetite and spirit, Amy must give greater energy to what spirit can offer and become more optimistically oriented towards that, rather than towards the risks and rewards that she is putting at the forefront of her awareness.

Much like Walter, Amy has a choice:

- She could rationalize her situation through a model of interpretation that causes her to feel and/or think in specific ways, meaning she could continue to feel 'dissed' by her client or
- She could include herself in the very next moment by giving away the conspiracy that refuses mutuality and trust. To protect, discern and confirm *that,* Amy will need to confront her insecurity, by a greater flexibility that can tolerate resentment.

After much discussion with the client, a delay in the campaign was announced. The client did not feel entirely ready. Amy felt that by leaving the door open for a delay, she gained an important insight. Resentment was an early warning indicator. If she blamed the client for apparent distrust, she most likely blamed herself for that as well. She did not have to see eye to eye, but discovering what the client want always helped her to manage her resentment.

To many, the economic model with its emphasis on probability, resource and outcome epitomizes the main features of rationality and reason. Rationality is necessary because choices have consequences. If we want to shape the outcomes we face, then measuring probability and consequence maybe the only way we can generate *that kind* of utility.

But how do we evaluate appetite and spirit?

Appetite and spirit are like the yin and yang inside our decision-making. Though difficult to isolate and identify, they are, nonetheless, present. The more we enmesh them *with reason*, the more likely we are to create an inhumane monster that refuses mutuality.

The power inside your decision making comes from choosing to be zanshin. The more you can shake off the hidden limitations that you carry, the more flexible you will become. But to do this, you must make room for the remaining mind. Too much devotion given to protecting, discerning and confirming will organize appetite and spirit in a pre-determined way, denigrating the mutuality of interdependence by forcing someone to absorb a loss.

For Amy that loss was calibrated with resentment. For Walter it was calibrated with anger and frustration. For each, these early warning indicators distorted the interdependence they were hoping to find because these losses made the past both too real and too concrete.

It is easy to evaluate decisions in terms of either *de*pendence or *in*dependence. *De*pendence because the world forces us to work with the "given" nature of things, and *in*dependence because we are constantly making decisions that are unique to us. What is much harder to sustain is our appreciation for *inter*dependence. The conspiracy that energizes the bias blind spot is that we are isolated, separate and alone.

What gets sewn into time is a unique experience, one that merges subjective feeling with objective reality. That experience depends on willing trust that we have with ourselves. The question we must ask is: are we actually willing to trust any evaluation of duration, scope, and preference *when the future has yet to happen?*

This is why we must let go of the limitations of narrow logic. Reason extrapolates based on the past when the here-and-now moment *is different.* The good feeling, positive self-image, and level of confidence we had in the past may continue to inform us; however, the probabilities we draw from past experience must be considered *weakly* correlated to any ONE future outcome. Conditions of uncertainty, rationality and objective measurement are all secondary to the subjective "framing" of our experience. *Emotions matter—a lot.*

If we are caught by the frame, then we are likely to be limited by it. With too narrow a frame, what we protect, discern and confirm will be the world of our experience, no one else's.

Conclusion

Decision making can be viewed as a Utility Pendulum. We make decisions so that we can self-identify with our choices. Our first decision is how we deal with the arbitrary. We could default to rationalizing our situation through our old model of interpretation that causes us to feel and think in specific ways, or we could include ourselves on both sides of any decision and deal with the arbitrary in a more inclusive way.

If you move to the center of the pendulum swing, your decision making will be more effective and flexible. By becoming zanshin, you become more than you ever thought possible. Good feeling, positive self-image, and higher levels of confidence can motivate you to do great things.

Self-Help: The First Decision

This chapter offered several insights that may help you negotiate obstacles, pressures and fears that make it difficult to focus on a preference that you want to advocate for yourself.

Directions: To complete the following exercise, identify a situation that you had difficulty with, then see if the topics introduced in this chapter help you evaluate your situation differently.

Identify your problem situation here:

____

____

1. The Arbitrariness of Pressure

How likely is it that you were under pressure to discern or confirm what others were expecting?

Likely	**Not Likely**	**Unsure**
☐	☐	☐

2. Duration, Scope and Preference

How likely is it that you are exaggerating your situation based a limited point of view or based on a negative outcome?

Likely	**Not Likely**	**Unsure**
☐	☐	☐

3. The First Decision

How likely is it that you could willingly change your way of exaggerating (assuming you were exaggerating)?

Likely	**Not Likely**	**Unsure**
☐	☐	☐

4. Reason, Logic, Appetite and Spirit

If reason, logic, appetite and spirit are features of personality, how likely is it that you might actually "see" your situation in a completely different way?

Likely	**Not Likely**	**Unsure**
☐	☐	☐

5. The Utility Pendulum

If obstacles, pressures and fears make it difficult to focus on what *you* want, would greater flexibility be useful?

Useful	**Not Useful**	**Unsure**
☐	☐	☐

6. Illustrating the First Decision

If you could put yourself on the other side of whatever happens, would protection still be useful or even necessary?

Useful	**Not Useful**	**Unsure**
☐	☐	☐

CHAPTER 3:

Personal Agency

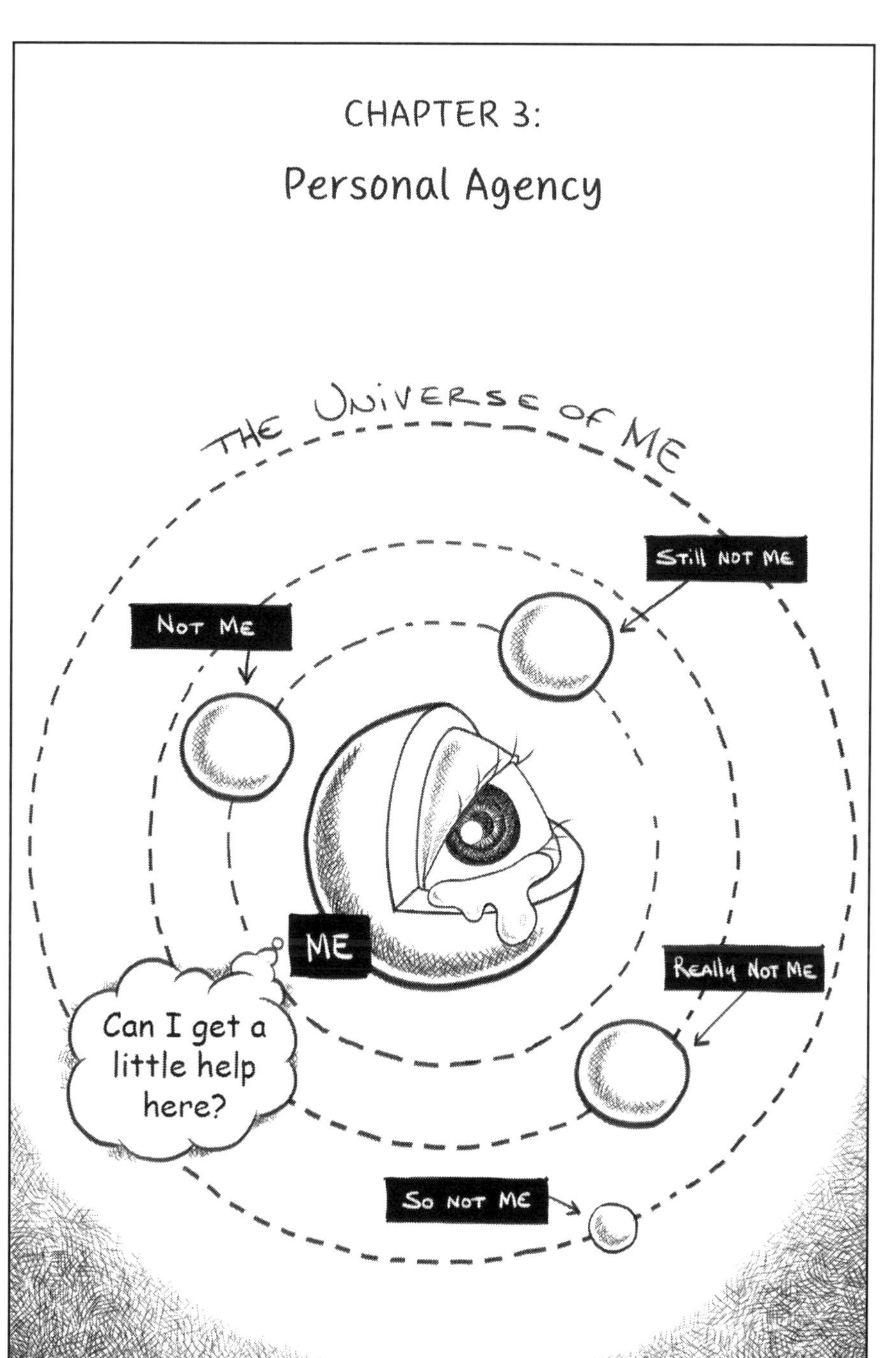

CHAPTER 3: Personal Agency

The personal "Universe of ME" is an interesting place. The good feeling, self-image and confidence we have is buried inside the centermost "ME-planet," but what we might notice first is all the *NOT ME* planets. Too much attention on them makes it hard to identify what we want.

NOT ME planets are commitments that have a negative utility (that is, they represent choices you don't like, choices that make you uncomfortable, or they represent actions you cannot take). You push them away, but you can't get rid of them. When there are too many of them, your personal universe soon becomes unmanageable. Stress, fatigue and sadness replace the good feeling, self-image and confidence you might otherwise have.

The question we must ask ourselves is: "Do I accept my current view of what is causing me pain, or do I work to change my way of seeing?" Which approach offers me the most help?

We make decisions, large and small, day-in and day-out. So when we cannot make those decisions confidently, we hurt. Asking for help is a reasonable, and even wise, thing to do.

In this chapter, we are going to look at the habits and routines that lead to how we protect and defend against the NOT ME planets. When good feeling, self-image and confidence fall by the wayside, we sometimes are left feeling a bit like a monster. There is a contrapasso[7], or suffering of the opposite, that occurs simply by choosing to maintain an agreed upon routine. That's why we look to others for support. We cannot sustain the good feeling,

7 Contrapasso refers to behavior directed more by what is feared than by what is desired. Here, a feared opposite creates a rigidity that occupies one's attention.

self-image and confidence we want if the actions of others appear arbitrary or offensive.

We deal with it by talking about it.

Sometimes a default personality takes over. Hopefully, that personality can be encouraged to let go of self-protection. However, that desire is often centered on the past and outcomes that led us to create NOT ME planets in the first place. Talk definitely helps, but in the end it all comes back to us.

To be "an agent" is to act on the basis of your power and to give it focus. Personal Agency is *you*, the possessor of reason, logic, appetite and spirit. We have everything we need, but can we choose to use that power in a way that is helpful when we are so negatively persuaded by everything around us? Not an easy task.

In the last chapter, you were introduced to the terms that define Personal Agency:

- **Reason** governs your awareness for time and its impact.
- **Logic** is how you organize that awareness.
- **Appetite** is a worldly desire for sensory experience.
- **Spirit** is the perennial desire for growth and transformation.

All of these influence your decision making, however, none is more instrumental than your defaults—that is, the choices you make without even knowing that you make them. Personal Agency starts with our defaults, and more specifically, with our habit of having a *definite* opinion about almost everything.

Personal Agency looks forward to outcomes. However, the more negative the outcome, the more energy we expend. *When we are zanshin with Personal Agency, we make a conscious choice to look at our habits and defaults before we engage with outcomes.* To be zanshin, we must reconsider the defaults that reason, logic, appetite and spirit are generating as pre-decisions. Maybe that way, we can find relief from the suffering of too many opposites and too much negativity.

Unquestioned Feeling

Our social media requires a mutual understanding.

At first, default decisions are based on how things *feel*. Without further reflection, we are likely to develop a whole series of unconscious habits. It's not that we cannot trust our feelings, but unless we have questioned them repeatedly, we are likely to soothe whatever irritating itch happens to grab hold of our attention.

Nobody's "social media" understanding is attuned to every situation, so arriving at a mutual understanding requires letting go of our pre-occupations, whether that be potential elation on the one side, or a deep dismay on the other.

Consider an extremely intelligent student, Anthony, who is struggling with a problem. When he asks his professor for help, the professor smiles, says nothing and leaves the room. Anthony perhaps *feels* many things. Perhaps he feels slighted, ignored, angry, embarrassed or humiliated. Because of Anthony's unconscious habits, he now questions his very intelligence and begins to lose confidence in his scholastic ability because his habitual pattern is to pile on self-criticism and self-doubt. Sound at all familiar?

Let me share a Zen wisdom story.

Worse than a Clown

There was a young monk in China who was a very serious practitioner of Buddhism.

Once, this monk came across something he did not understand, so he went to ask the master. When the master heard the question, he kept laughing. The master then stood up and walked away, still laughing.

The young monk was very disturbed by the master's reaction. For the next three days, the young monk could not eat, sleep nor think properly. At the end of three days, he went back to the master and told the master how disturbed he had felt.

When the master heard this, he said, "Monk, do you know what your problem is? Your problem is that YOU ARE WORSE THAN A CLOWN!"

The monk was shocked to hear that, "Venerable Sir, how can you say such a thing?! How can I be worse than a clown?"

The master explained, "A clown enjoys seeing people laugh. You? You feel disturbed because another person laughed. Tell me: are you not worse than a clown?"

When the monk heard this, he began to laugh. He was enlightened.[8]

Our most common default is to take things personally. The mind tends to conjure up negative associations more quickly than positive ones. The itch that has our attention is often some repetition of a bad experience. We make the current situation into a trigger about the past. How different would Anthony's response have been if he decided to view what happened as an impersonal and isolated event, disconnected from anything in his past? Instead of defaulting to instant self-doubt, perhaps the situation could be explained by something as simple as the professor did not hear his question. The professor's behavior could be due to many things that had nothing at all to do with Anthony. How would your life be if you could operate from this understanding?

Zanshin Observation: People are unaware of how personally they take comments and criticism. If you never question the itch that makes criticism difficult for you, you will not be zanshin.

8 An almost verbatim copy of the story can be found at http://www.whatdoyouthinkmyfriend.com/Stories/clown.html

The Rigidity of Habits

Don't panic, I'm just a "little habit."

When we first step into Personal Agency, our decisions are primarily about soothing the itch that has our attention. "Little habits," we call them. Seemingly harmless, they visit our doors often enough that we no longer give them any attention.

We are unconsciously drawn to the routine patterns that help us "habituate" to our environment. The more resistant those habits are, the more we will adopt a fixed rigidity. To be more zanshin, you must cultivate an awareness that can hold the tension between the logic you use with your pre-decisions and the reason, appetite and spirit that can offer greater access to what's going on. By itself, logic does not create a wall between yourself and others. Only the desire to protect a fixed way of being can do that. That's when all the "little habits" become so very hard to overcome.

Here is a short story that illustrates this point:

Habitual Cheat

There once was a man who behaved like a cheat, encouraging people to think he was a holy man so they might give him money. Of course, he didn't originally plan to be a cheat; however, he was first mistaken as a holy man because of an accident. In his youth, he was shipwrecked and washed ashore completely naked. He tied a piece of bark to his body and went around begging for food. The plight of his poverty seemed so clearly spiritual to others that they thought he was holy man.

For a time, the man survived quite happily on the money of others and even he started to believe that he really was a holy man. This went on until one night he had a dream. God gave him a scolding for what he was doing. The man decided he wanted to change, so he sought out a genuine holy man for advice.

The holy man saw into his soul and realized that the cheating man had created a wall between himself and others. The cheat had created a habit that encouraged him to believe the most superficial and self-centered things. The genuine holy man proposed the following scriptural verse to pacify his need to cheat:

> "Where there is seeing, there is only the seeing, there is no see-er. Where there is listening, there is only the listening, there is no listen-er. Where there is feeling, there is only the feeling, and so on."

It was a very profound verse. But as the cheat left, he said to the holy man, "What am I going to think about if I don't take my all my needs seriously?" And, once again, the cheat became completely naked.[9]

This story offers many potential insights. The Buddhist scripture verse encourages us to disbelieve our senses. Why? Because too much belief leads to exaggerated illusions and habits. Appetite is generally the most habit forming when it combines with memory, then some part of reason, logic and spirit flows along with appetite to make our

---

9 (Modified). Based on a traditional Zen story; see http://www.whatdoyouthinkmyfriend.com/Stories/bahiya.html.

beliefs difficult to overcome. After all, you are what you think. Who doesn't want to trust one's senses?

However, the more you focus on the illusion of separation, the more you will cheat yourself of life's beauty. Nakedness is often portrayed as both a physical and a spiritual quality. To become naked is to return to an original condition, which may signal a continuing repetition or a breakthrough to something altogether different. In the traditional ending of this story, the cheat becomes enlightened and loses his addiction to sensory awareness because he is "finally ready." With that ending, the return to an original condition is more spiritual than physical. With the current ending, the return is a reiteration of the default which the cheat always uses. That desire to self-protect can be hard to overcome. Our default is sometimes the only thing we know how to take seriously.

Zanshin Observation: People often do not see how they cheat themselves by over protecting. To be zanshin is to not limit yourself in this way.

Opinions and Judgements

Thank God! A panel of experts!

Feelings translate into opinions and judgements. While there are both good and bad things that can be said about this, the fact is we must harness and use our opinions and judgements if we are going to decide anything at all.

Much of the time it can feel like we are crawling out of the desert because it is hard to trust our routines once we've started to question them.

Reason, logic, appetite and spirit give shape and meaning to even minor evaluations. Reason draws out consequence, logic organizes what we decide, while appetite and spirit yield satisfaction and connection. To make a decision with Personal Agency, we must give some attention to all four. But logic and our tendency to pre-decide can make this difficult.

When formulating opinions and judgements, we primarily draw upon reason. We must acknowledge our situation, evaluate our remembrance of the past and then decide what we expect to see happen in the future. Because the future is so hard to determine, the panel of experts we crave is primarily concerned about the future.

Every future can be permanent or temporary in **duration**; every future can be pervasive or limited in **scope**; and every future can be especially worthy and truthful, or meaningless and irrelevant in its **preferential feeling**. The feelings generated by these evaluations are all composites of actual experience. They remind us of everything we have been through so that we can move toward something that is better than what we have experienced already.

Reason's first impulse is to associate consequence using everything we remember about the past. When an experience is sewn into time, we associate the past with the present so it can hold meaning for us. For example, Anthony, that very intelligent student we met earlier, had a father who used to ignore his questions because they were "too stupid" to bother with. Anthony's default association was to use the past to clarify the present.

Like Anthony, we must decide: Is this possible future going to be a ME event or a NOT ME event? Will this add to my good feeling, self-image and confidence or diminish them? If it does diminish them, must I create a fearful NOT ME planet just to protect my way of being in the world?

There is no objective measure for this judgement. Our evaluation is entirely subjective. We can agree to share a common perspective; however, the decision to agree must always remain with the individual. This is why opinions and judgements matter so much. If the future is an extension of the present and if we are invested in trying to "make more" by "doing better," then we must use good feeling, self-image and confidence to bring greater awareness to the future that we are deciding right now. Reason is a grinding mill "pre-decider." It transforms our experience so we can understand the person we are trying to become. However, if we *only* self-protect, we will never learn how much we actually *do* share with others. Too much self-congratulation given to our judgements and opinions can lead to even greater anxiety and separation, not less. Isolation is the banishment borne of too much self-protection.

This next story illustrates the importance of our opinions and judgements and how they must be focused on "making more" by "doing better."

The Rooster or the Prince?

A long time ago, there lived a handsome and intelligent prince; however, one morning it got into the prince's head that he was a rooster. This opinion became an obsession and soon he took off all his clothes and lived under the dining room table flapping his arms and crowing, just like a rooster. His father, the king, was deeply saddened by this behavior. The king called in his best doctors, miracle workers, and magicians to see what could be done. One by one, each tried as best as they could to help the prince, but to no avail. The prince continued to believe he was a rooster.

The king fell into depression, unhappily resigning himself to the idea that no one would be able to cure his son of his strange malady. Until one day, a peculiar sage arrived with a weird message: "To pull a man out of the mud, a friend must set foot into that mud." The king pondered the message and the more he thought about it, the more it made sense. The king agreed to let this sage try to help his son.

To everyone's amazement, the sage took off all his clothes and joined the prince under the dining room table, flapping his arms and crowing like a rooster. "What are you doing?" asked the prince.

"Can't you see," said the sage, "I'm a rooster just like you."

The prince was overjoyed to have a new friend and after a short while, he came to admire him more and more. One day, the sage got out from under the table and stretched his back and stood up.

"What are you doing?" asked the prince.

"Don't worry," said the sage. "Just because you are a rooster doesn't mean that you cannot temporarily stand up."

The prince followed along and stood up and stretched. It was true: a rooster can stand up and stretch and still be a rooster. If you prefer to feel like a rooster, you can. "That way you can 'make more' of who you are by 'doing better' with what you've been given," said the sage.

The next day, the sage put on his shirt and pants. The prince looked at him and said, "Are you crazy? Roosters don't wear clothes."

The sage said, "I was a little chilled. Besides, just because you are a rooster doesn't mean that you cannot be made warmer by wearing clothes. It's just a limited sort of change. You are still a rooster."

The next day, while standing up and wearing clothing, the sage sat down at the table and started to eat just like other people. The prince jumped up and exclaimed, "Don't you realize we are roosters!?! How can we be sitting at a table eating and talking just like we were men?"

> The sage said, "Here is a great secret. You can dress like a man, eat like a man and talk like a man and still remain a rooster. All these temporary changes are just limited adjustments."[10]

The "stories" we tell ourselves about the past have an indelible impact on how we evaluate the present. But, so too does the way we perceive ourselves. The more we give into habits and defaults, the more we use reason, logic, appetite and spirit to repeat an established pattern. To "make more" by "doing better" requires a different way of thinking, which is all about staying in the center of the pendulum swing. Too much to an extreme … and who knows? You might become either a prince or a rooster. The benefit of the Zanshin Middle Path is that you are open to seeing the world in a new way.

> **Zanshin Observation:** People do not acknowledge the duration, scope, and preference they create; they see it as part of who they are. If you do this too rigidly, you cannot be zanshin.

Greater Awareness

10 (Heavily modified). Based on the story "Prince Rooster" by Nina Jaffe and Steve Zeitlin, *While Standing on One Foot: Puzzle Stories and Wisdom Tales from the Jewish Tradition*, Henry Holt and Company, New York, 1993, pp. 70-75.

Are you undecided? If you want to be zanshin, you might feel *open-endedly* undecided. Here, you are neither apathetic nor uninformed—but still willing to be persuaded as the situation presents itself. Like this guy on his cell phone, we can learn to defy the expectations of others if we are willing.

The reasoning that springs out of our evaluation of *duration, scope* and *preference* is intuitive and only partially self-aware. Our good feeling, self-image and level of confidence are constantly being re-evaluated as we compare past to present and present to future. By engaging in what happens around us, we bring forward a pattern of awareness that, potentially, can "make more" by "doing better." However, to implement that desire requires planning and organization. This is why we must confront the logic we use. It is fine to say, "*This* is permanent and unchanging while *that* is not," but unless a person *does* something with that awareness, it will have little or no direct impact. If we do not construct a world that builds upon the distinctions that are alive for us, we will remain separate and removed from ourselves. So logic helps us to make use of what we perceive, the key point being that it does so as long as we do not become *overinvested*; the logic that organizes our decisions, can, does and *will* change.

Logic implements various rules to insure consistency in our planning and organization. With comprehensive logic, we become more aware of ourselves and our impact on others. In contrast, *partial* logic creates unanticipated vulnerability. When this happens, we are surprised by our own inconsistency. For example, if we gossip about others but are offended when others gossip about us, we may find that contradiction hard to accept. That "logical" inconsistency creates vulnerability, leading to stronger resistance and even greater stress.

Partial logic is like a raw wound that never heals. We keep revisiting it hoping to solve the contradiction. That is one reason why we create unnecessary suffering. We cannot grasp the full logic of what we are doing, and there *is* hope. Any overinvestment can simply be redirected. There's nothing wrong with distracting ourselves from an overbearing obsession.

The Seven Logics shown below are posted widely across the Internet. They illustrate how you can "make more" by "doing better" when you have a general rule of thumb to search for any default inconsistency. The way we apply these logics to the future we want lessens that wall of separation created by what we pre-decide.

1. Make peace with your past so it doesn't spoil your present.
2. What others think of you is none of your business.
3. Time heals almost everything, so give time some time.
4. No one is the reason of your happiness except YOU yourself.
5. Don't compare your life with the lives of others. You have no idea what their journey is all about.
6. Stop thinking too much; it's all right not to know all the answers.
7. Smile. You don't own all the problems in the world.

Each of these statements represents a practice of Personal Agency that will help you negotiate the middle ground between the ME | NOT ME extremes. The more you use Personal Agency to let go of any exaggerated habits and defaults, the easier it is to be zanshin. The goal is to be aware of your circumstances while at the same time, be uncommitted to any outcome or condition. The gameshow contestant may want to win a million dollars; however, one clear obstacle is the critical voice that exaggerates the immediacy of what might happen. You must always have some place to cross *to* once an event is over. Finding a SAFE place on both sides changes the way you make a decision. You don't feel so hemmed in. With protection on both sides, your response becomes an option. You can be positive and *open-endedly* undecided without being apathetic or uninformed. The seven logics make this possible.

Let me expound a bit on each:

1. The past is a representational default—what that means is we cannot represent anything without having some knowledge of it. The more we build representations based on the past, the

more we will repeat the most habitual associations. That, in turn, accentuates whatever impact the past may have. Just knowing alleviates a great burden.

2. Comparative evaluation is a representational default. It requires a qualitative scale. The more you give awareness to the scale, the more you will be invested in a specific outcome or condition.
3. Time creates a qualitative distance and affords a greater awareness of continuity. With more time, the scale of impact between ME | NOT ME diminishes. What hurt in the past almost never hurts to the same degree now, provided we give "time" some time. Awareness doesn't mean reliving the past.
4. Happiness might seem to be more present and available out near the extremes of ME | NOT ME, but happiness actually has greater color and nuance when you are more safely placed somewhere near the middle. To be zanshin is to be SAFE: Stable, Adaptive, Flexible, and Energized, which you cannot find out there at the extremes.
5. A lifetime is more than a moment and a journey is most certainly *not* a destination. If you are aware and uncommitted to any specific outcome, you will more easily accept the need for all journeys, *and* you will never feel alone or abandoned if your journey is allowed to express its own potential. That way, your journey can potentially build upon the journey of others.
6. If you identify a Problem (with a capital P), you are establishing an awareness that requires personal attention. If you use too much Personal Agency to find the one and only "right" answer, you might potentially be overwhelmed. Personalizing an outcome exaggerates its impact.
7. There are other domains besides the domain of Personal Agency; respecting that will alleviate the need to "own" all of the world's problems.

Here is a short story about the importance of logic and how we can always make changes to it.

Accepting Life's Logic

The ancient Japanese Zen Master, Hikaru, overheard his family complaining how his nephew was wasting money on prostitutes and high living. Hikaru listened silently, without comment, and then went to visit his nephew, whom he had not seen for many years.

His nephew invited Hikaru to stay the night. All night long, Hikaru sat in meditation while his nephew watched from a distance. The next morning as he prepared to go, Hikaru said, "I must be getting old. I have no strength in my hands. Will you help me tie the string for my sandals?"

The nephew did as he was asked.

Hikaru replied, "Thank you. A man becomes older and more enfeebled every day. Take care of yourself."

Hikaru left. He never said a word about the prostitutes or the high living. But from that day on, his nephew truly reformed. He stopped putting his energy into dissipating his life. [11]

If you consider how the nephew's life was changed, you see that all Seven Logics were at work in some way. The past does not control the present; what others think is none of your business; time heals; no one is the reason for your happiness but you; don't compare; stop obsessing about answers; and smile. Hikaru's nephew did not have to own everyone else's problem, just his own.

---

11 (Slightly modified). Based on a traditional Zen story; see http://www.whatdoyouthinkmyfriend.com/Stories/ryokanslesson.html.

Zanshin Observation: People who are zanshin move through life's logic without clinging to specific judgements; they appreciate life moments without dissipating their energies needlessly.

The Pressure of Appetite

Few love to hear the sin which they, themselves, might act.

Much of what complicates life is appetite and our desire for sensory experience. It often keeps us awake at night contemplating things with a combination of envy and regret.

It's not just that we want to feel our place in the world, but we also want to be sated by that experience. Satiety means fulfillment. When we are completely full, we no longer seek after the temporary pleasure that an experience provides. So, however temporary or prolonged one's experience may be, the impact that satiety creates is strongly felt. Over time, we regulate our activities based on a drive to get more of the same. The pressure any appetite creates is largely repetitive. We keep returning to a familiar set of routines that offer us the promise of satiety, which, surprisingly enough, doesn't change all that much.

What psychologists refer to as "the hedonic treadmill" is the tendency for individuals—no matter what their temporary experience—to quickly return to a relatively stable level of happiness. Major life events are folded into a person's overall experience and people will generally return to the same level of fulfillment where they started. Even if our game show contestant had won the million dollars, his ecstasy would be temporary and he would return to his "normal" level of happiness. Many lottery winners end up broke and unhappy, if that is how life "felt" to them prior to winning their jackpots. Major life events do not have a long-term impact; however, the way we anticipate (or avoid) major life events does. The suffering we go through can equal the suffering of Job, if we are incessantly prompted to avoid or fight just to stay even.

With most any appetite (be that, food, shelter, clothing, money, status) we generally believe "things just aren't good enough." The brain is wired to vividly remember negative events. The pressure we feel around our appetites is predicated *not* by the relatively stable level of happiness to which we return, but rather, by the heightened anticipation that one day we will be short-changed in our efforts to "make more" by "doing better." Few love to hear the sin which they might act because we are fearful of our own vulnerability. Appetite can be very insistent.

If the future is an extension of the present and if we are completely invested in our effort to "make more" by "doing better" than no matter what did happened *in the past,* our first association is likely be negative, not positive. Most people are not optimistically pre-disposed. We vividly remember the slights and snubs without remembering how unimportant they are in the long run.

Because of that, trusting the Middle Path can be pretty hard, even though over the long haul we *do* return to the middle. Most people have a tendency to behave in a very clown-like fashion: we anticipate the worst and then are surprised when, all of a sudden, the worst doesn't happen. If we want to be zanshin, it's not that we do not acknowledge our appetites, it's just that we do not immediately buy into the exaggerated future forecast that creates an unquestioned giddiness (at getting more than we expect) or an unquestioned sadness (at the idea of being denied our satisfaction). The trick is to use our awareness of duration, scope and preference to stay the course. The good feeling, self-image, and confidence that combine together are more flexible than we assume.

Here is a story that illustrates the disproportionate nature of our appetites and our inability to realistically predict what may or may not happen when we act on them.

The Greedy Monkey

A Zen teacher took his pupils out into the forest to a clearing known to have wild monkeys. There he placed a hollow gourd with a narrow opening. Since he wanted to attract the monkeys so his students could observe them, he placed honey sweetened rice into the gourd (a monkey favorite). Next, he secured the gourd to a strong metal stick and waited with his class.

Soon, a very large monkey approached. Being curious, he sniffed the rice and then inserted his paw. Unfortunately, the monkey discovered he could not withdraw his paw (now a fist) through the gourd's narrow opening. He howled and howled with frustration.

Just then a tiger approached. Having heard the loud noise, the tiger decided to have monkey for dinner.

"Let go of the rice," screamed the pupils. "Run!" But to no avail. The monkey, in his hunger, refused to let go of the rice and as a result, was eaten by the tiger.

On the way home, the master asked, "What was the trap that killed the monkey?"

"Rice," said one student. "The gourd," said another.

"No," replied the wise teacher. "The trap was insatiable greed."[12]

---

12 (Lightly modified). Based on a traditional Zen story; see http://read.goodweb.cn/PDF/p33/101%20Zen%20stories.pdf.

> **Zanshin Observation:** Appetite is insatiable if we are predisposed to look at the negative experience of loss. Every appetite clamors for instant gratification, so too much attention on that pressure will make it harder to be zanshin.

Our Connection to Spirit

The pressure of appetite is constant, but what springs from the spirit is larger and more cohesive than we imagine.

Much of what feels enjoyable has to do with our perennial desire for growth and transformation: our first kiss, our first home, our first job. None of these might seem particularly spiritual; however, if you consider how these events connect us to a larger world, then the spiritual dimensions become much more poignant and clear.

While one's appetite repeats, leading us to normalize with a predictable pattern, the engagement we have with growth and transformation does not. We are forever discovering and re-discovering how we participate in a world that is expansively larger than we could imagine. Life is a never-ending sewing together of myriad connections which are both strengthened—and weakened—by the way life unfolds.

It's important to remember: growth and transformation are often tenuous. Duration, scope and preference are always fitted to our personalities, however, given the pressures and anxieties we face, it's hard to trust, so what accompanies each new connection is a new pattern of trust that we must first bring about *in ourselves.*

If we feel isolated and burdened, we may need to develop strength and resilience. But how can we do that? Trust transforms the way we behave, yet these transitions are not easy, for wherever we find connection, we will also find vulnerability. We like to think that vulnerability can be "reasonably" accommodated, provided we impose enough distance between the risk we feel and the actual loss that might happen. However, to impose too much distance deadens our connection. The default *in*consistency that lends logic to our actions unconsciously keeps us in the driver's seat. We want full credit and full license to decide as *we* want, never realizing that by being so one-sided, we don't really trust others, or really, even ourselves. Full credit and full license is a nice idea when we are gunning for a specific result, but it can be disastrous when things don't go as we expect. The teacher who betrays the pupil will have no standing from which to teach. The tenuousness of our position is how unconsciously we hide from our own vulnerabilities, not realizing how inconsistent they can be.

The classic spiritual problem is losing trust once the world shortchanges our efforts. The never-ending dark days that cast a bleak pall over our bright world make distrust seem inevitable. The more we try, the less organized the future seems to us. Abandoned and in pain, it seems only right that we withhold trust. But the spiritual dimension is never entirely logical or consistent. Sure, we can "rethink" what we are doing, but more importantly we must re-organize the good feeling, self-image and confidence we never lost. Vulnerabilities are often driven by personality, but the spiritual dimension we carry is larger and more expansive than personality. We can set aside our vulnerabilities without at the same time denying that we have them.

To be more zanshin, we must loosen our grip on wanting too much distance or clinging to every decision because we were given full credit and full license to do so. The driver's seat is no guarantee against loss but it can be a great place of learning. Provided we stay in the Zanshin Overlap—difficult as that is.

Unless *you* choose happiness, you will wait forever for it. Unless you let go of your past, you will never know the present. Unless you drop your self-protective defense, you will never be SAFE, nor will you genuinely know safety. Unless *you* bring a new intention that risks everything, the outcome you experience will always be the same. We are often trapped by self-protecting expectations—the same NOT ME planets that drain us of energy and optimism. Distance itself does not create safety; it merely deadens the possibility of loss, given what we already think *will* happen.

In our connection to spirit there is always *maybe.* Never give away your maybes.

> **Zanshin Observation:** Spirit is open-ended provided we are predisposed to act with positive expectation and without guarantee. If you are hardened by a need for instant gratification, you cannot become zanshin.

Trust (and by extension, gratitude) guide us down the path of spiritual connection, yet often we bury trust by putting ourselves to sleep. Then again, this may be what the remaining mind does when we are happy and content for then we are not trying to deaden the pain of loss.

You may be familiar with the following often-quoted nugget.

> It is said that when Buddha was first enlightened, he was asked,
> "Are you a god?"
> "No," he replied.
> "Are you a saint?"
> "No."

"Then what are you?"

And he answered, "I am awake."[13]

Zanshin Observation: People who are zanshin move through the moment awakened by trust. We need not be gods or saints to trust genuinely or whole-heartedly.

Working at the Gut Level

If we put everything we "are" into what we "do," it may cause us to feel overwhelmed. It's hard to stay neutral or uncommitted, especially when others might abandon you. The thrill of victory and the agony of defeat are relative to the support and encouragement we find, not just in ourselves, but in others, too.

Personal Agency is like a rapidly spinning top that can push aside all manner of interference. It runs on reason, logic, appetite and spirit. To be inclusive (and zanshin), your decisions must stay present in the moment and not drift too much to either the past or

---

13 (Not modified). Based on a traditional Zen story; http://www.whatdoyouthinkmyfriend.com/Stories/awake.html.

the future. To build strength and confidence to deal with unforeseen hardships, you must learn to work at a gut level. But the gut level cannot be arbitrarily directed by the Pendulum extremes, otherwise, you will be like Charlie Chaplin's "Tramp" character. Yes, we are all governed by a degree of imaginary license to see the world as we want; however, when our actions impact others, then we must moderate our defenses so they may join us and help us (assuming that is what we genuinely want). Enhanced interdependence and integration is built on flexibility and trust. The "Tramp" character is funny because he is ironically self-absorbed. He trusts in ways that illustrate a loss of connection that we all understand because, like him, we often lose sight of our resistance. Duration, scope and preference bring the world closer to us and no matter how much we are overwhelmed by fear, we never really lose that.

So, what does it mean to work at the gut level?

- To be so deeply involved in what you want to accomplish that the only thing that matters is doing your best. (The thrill and agony cannot create durable or lasting motivation.)
- To direct your care and concern to each stage, step and process without becoming distracted by minor annoyances or extraneous thoughts. (To use a focused awareness without drifting into obsession.)
- To give of yourself patiently and freely—with lightly held pride. (Nothing we do is exclusively for ourselves.)
- To be clear about your goals and about what you must do to accomplish them *and* to be ready to make any necessary adjustment to sustain forward momentum. (Only the gut will tell you when you have gone too far either way.)
- To bring curiosity and enthusiasm to the work at hand so it may be a pleasure throughout. (Personal Agency does not go well without good feeling and pleasure.)

When we are successful with the above, Personal Agency demonstrates assurance that can be an inspirational source of strength to others. Imagine how deeply satisfying this way of working can be. Remember, the gut rules the measure. We may *intend* to use Personal Agency as I have described, yet many things can interfere. The four things that most get in our way include: (1) fear and guilt, (2) choosing to hold back, (3) unproductive duplicity and lying, and (4) lack of creativity.

Fear and Guilt

Starting something new is unsettling. We may anticipate obstacles and limits, which, in turn, create fear or perhaps even guilt if success is unwelcome or uncomfortable for others. If we become too much afraid, we may withdraw and fail to use our best efforts. We may become easily distracted and disengage because we associate our work with past experience or with a difficult comparative evaluation that requires the one "right" answer that cannot be easily found.

All of these can cause us to offer less of ourselves and even become distant or potentially aloof. We may find ourselves doing just the bare minimum. The unsettling nature of "the new" can cause us to become doubtful, to give only partial attention, to make unnecessary mistakes, to misinterpret communication, and to miss deadlines. Dissatisfaction like this can snowball, making the work an unpleasant duty when time hangs heavy and we are no longer aligned with what we are trying to accomplish. Fear and guilt can also lead us to self-sabotage by creating "gremlins" out of past habits and behaviors. Fear and guilt are two reasons why Personal Agency turns into a ME | NOT ME double bind. We refuse to let go of the intensity that constrains our more positive energy, yet in turn, that forces us to repeat our more familiar habits.

Choosing to Hold Back

When we choose to hold back, we may have decided that there is some loss that we cannot negotiate, or we harbor a belief that is pushing us into doubt or disbelief. By holding back, we become increasingly self-centered and take issue with tiny things that have no real bearing on our goal. We stop being zanshin because our Personal Agency has gotten stuck. Here, we might need to shift out of Personal Agency and move into a more Impersonal state where everything can be open-endedly questioned.

Holding back in this way is not necessarily a bad thing. We must remember how naked we are, how vulnerable. However, the more aware we are of personal vulnerability, the more that awareness can distort our sharing with others, thus limiting the freedom we might otherwise have.

Personal Agency is highly sensitive to all the potential triggers that cause us to be less than we want. Sometimes, it is better to hold back than to unnecessarily lash out or resist. How beautiful it is to stay silent when someone expects you to be enraged.

The ME | NOT ME double bind doesn't require *all* of our attention. Choosing to hold back in this way invites a kind of reflection that enables us to adopt a more moderate state of engagement. Working at the gut level of Personal Agency is not a constant forward march. So take a break now and then.

Good listening requires that we hold back and appraise the moment by attending with "whole body" awareness. High practitioners of open-ended listening gain insight from the entirety of what happens. So choosing to hold back is an important way to shift out of a more directive style of Personal Agency, provided we are aware of it.

Holding back really *only* becomes a problem whenever we are working with loss or feel completely overwhelmed by what we are trying to accomplish. With zanshin awareness, we can slip into varying patterns of engagement without committing to any one outcome or result. That's normally enough to put us back on track.

Unproductive Duplicity and Lying

Sometimes our Personal Agency becomes so confused that we fall into various types of duplicity and lying. When we hold ourselves in a superior position relative to others, we often feel justified to create euphemisms, either to conceal our dissatisfactions and conflicts or to make an end run around them. Holding our pain and joy in secret is not just the antics of the clown. Social pressure demands protection. We conspire with duration, scope and preference to over-commit by playing loose with what is factually true (both for us and for others).

If you stay in the Zanshin Overlap, then illusion-making euphemisms and lies are easier to acknowledge and identify. But the distorting effect of diminished good feeling, self-image and confidence must also be taken into account. With too much loss, we mask the dissonance that we might otherwise recognize thus making it easier to lie even to ourselves. A desired illusion can become captivatingly real. Denial and stonewalling are extreme examples of the selective blindness of NOT ME engagement. Loss can be very difficult to accommodate.

If we work at the gut level with zanshin awareness, then reason, logic, appetite and spirit (the components of personality) are less likely to be overrun with unproductive energy. However, the decision utility we seek cannot be of a zero-sum nature. Economic choices are calculated to bury interpersonal tensions. If we are given full credit and full license to make a decision, we want to know that we are joining *with* others—not merely working against them. Pressure, obstacles and fear are all part of the zero-sum game of wanting specific outcomes. Duplicity and lying are simply the avoidance of relationship and are based solely on self-protection. We still want to believe that distance equals safety.

Lack of Creativity

Working at the gut level requires creativity. Using the resources of time, intelligence, curiosity, and empathy (which all play into creativity) requires that our Personal Agency be more open-ended than closed. Imagination comes into play whenever two people come together. The way we interact and share our mental resources cannot be algorithmically patterned or determined in advance. When we lack creativity, we assume that problems are of limited complexity, and therefore, open to simple solutions. Interdependence is not a simple endeavor. Anticipation and enthusiasm are necessary springboards that will, most often, release creativity. The more openly we value these, the more our Personal Agency will flourish with a combination of nuance and depth. If we are pinned down or railroaded by an extreme, that often forces us to take up an extreme as well. Utility is a relationship, not an outcome. Creativity embraces that basic idea more than any other mental faculty we have. Nothing can be specifically patterned in advance and everything must be negotiated.

The most zanshin forms of Personal Agency will occupy the Zanshin Overlap. Here, the extremes will inform, but not constrain, our choices as we look for opportunity. The surprise we discover is that even in the face of hardship hope flourishes. We face many complexities when trying to stay in that space but it is, nonetheless, always possible.

Working at the gut level is the most effective place we can occupy. However, we cannot successfully occupy the space of interpersonal (and personal) effectiveness if we are battling the habits that keep us involved with the ME | NOT ME extremes.

Here is a story that illustrates some of the difficulties we have when trying to work at the gut level.

The Man Who Planted Dates

Off in a faraway desert, Bassam, an octogenarian nearing the end of his life, could be found planting dates in a particularly fertile oasis.

Ashraf, a much younger friend and neighbor, approached Bassam who was now sweating heavily in the afternoon sun.

Ashraf asked, "How goes it, old man? Peace be with you."

"And also with you," said Bassam.

"What are you doing out in this heat holding a shovel?" the neighbor inquired.

"I'm planting," said the old man.

"What are you planting, Bassam?"

"Dates," exclaimed Bassam, pointing to all the dates around him.

"Dates," repeated Ashraf in disbelief. He paused momentarily and thought, Surely this is the stupidest idea—an old man planting dates in the middle of the day! "Come Bassam, stop what you are doing and let's get a drink. I'll be happy to buy you one."

"No, I must finish planting. After that we can have a drink together."

"Look, my friend, dates take over fifty years to grow, and only when they become adult palms are they able to bear fruit. You don't expect to see any of that fruit, do you? Put down your shovel and come, there's nothing here for you."

"Look, Ashraf, I've eaten the dates sown by someone before me who also had no hope of eating those dates himself. Today I plant so that tomorrow, others can eat the dates I planted. Even if it is just to honor one stranger, it's worth my finishing this task."

"What made you decide that now was the time to do this?" asked Ashraf.

"I have known fear and guilt most of my life, so much that I have chosen not to give very much of myself. I have been holding back for many, many years. I told myself that my contributions don't matter that much, that no one would notice, or that it would be impossible for me to really make a difference. Then yesterday, I passed this small date grove and realized that all of that was a mistake. When I closed my eyes, I saw the most beautiful thing: a date grove that I helped to plant and with every plant that flowered and grew, I was adding something to the enjoyment of others. Now do you understand?"

> "Yes, Bassam, you have taught me a great lesson. Let me pay you for that lesson with this stack of coins." And as he spoke, he placed a small sack in the old man's hands.
>
> "Ashraf, you are too kind. I never expected to reap anything from what I sowed here, on this day. I'm not even done with my planting and I already have reaped a sack of coins and the gratitude of a friend. But Ashraf, all you really need to do is buy me a drink once I am done. That will be thanks enough."
>
> And just as the sun went down, the two men could be seen sharing a drink while laughing at the very foolishness of life. [14]

This story illustrates the fulfillment of the Middle Path. To reap what you sow is a metaphor that brings together inner and outer realms. (That is what Bassam was really planting: a wish for inner satisfaction.) The "very foolishness of life" is how we often mistake one for the other. (That is what Ashraf and Bassam were celebrating: the shared understanding of a life well lived).

We cannot *always* know the impact of our actions. Much of what we create with ambition results in an "unanswered ending," that is, an ending that leaves us holding questions rather than certainties. The good feeling, self-image, and level of confidence we have must expand what is possible for others—not only ourselves. I will have more to say about unanswered endings once we get to Divine Agency.

> **Zanshin Observation:** People who work at the gut level understand how challenging it can be to trust the larger picture. When you are zanshin, fulfillment still requires work; however, with even minor achievements you will discover gratitude.

---

14 (Modified). Based on the story, "The Man Who Planted Dates," by Dr. Jorge Bucay, PhD., *Let Me Tell You a Story: Tales along the road to Happiness*, Europa Editions, 2013, pp. 205-206.

Indecision and Personal Agency

Inner and the outer realities are difficult to manage. To work at the gut level requires a commitment that is easily dismissed if we are unwilling to accept the Middle Path.

Remember the observations that have been made in this chapter:

- People are unaware how personally they take comments and criticism.
- People often do not see how they cheat themselves when they take their needs too seriously.
- People do not acknowledge the duration, scope, and preference they create; instead, they see it as part of who they are.
- People who are zanshin move through life's logic without clinging to specific judgements.
- Appetite is insatiable if we are predisposed to look at the negative experience of loss.
- Spirit is open-ended provided we are predisposed to act with positive expectation and without a guarantee.
- People who are zanshin move through the moment awakened by trust. There is no limit to what trust might offer them.
- People who work at the gut level understand how challenging it is to trust the larger picture.

When you are zanshin, fulfillment is not necessarily easy, but you can realize it more and more of it with time and practice.

It is one thing to discover "utility" from a personal point of view; it is another to make "protection" the sole focus of your effort. Personal Agency tries to enforce a compensating distance over whatever is feared but without running away from it.

So, if you are facing a tough decision, what do you do?

- First, look at what has your attention. What makes this a tough decision? Not enough information? Mixed priorities? Past experience?

- What is the one thing that creates the most ambivalence? The potential of being judged? The uncertainty of the outcome? The amount of coordination required?

Now that you have some handle on your decision ambivalence, can you adopt a neutral perspective so you can explore what's at stake in a more directed way? It may not be easy but the benefits are many.

Personal Awareness and Direct Contemplation

Your default rationalizations and pre-decisions come from reason, logic, appetite and spirit. Try asking specific questions of each.

- How are you thinking about your situation?

By identifying the situational triggers, you may uncover potential options. The reason we feel ambivalent and indecisive is due to some awareness of risk or opportunity. We may hold two (or possibly more) distinct perspectives that vie for our attention. Each one may indicate the threat of risk or the promise of opportunity.

- Do you have a preference? Which preference holds opportunity? Which one holds risk? Why are you personally being pulled into the situation or thrown out of it?
- Do you have a presumption about duration? Which presumption is long-term? Which one is short-term? Do you feel a conflict between the two?
- Do you have a presumption about scope? Is one presumption more fearful or desirous than the other? Do you sense any conflict?

As you work with these questions, notice how the durability of good feeling can change, how your self-image shifts, and how your confidence can be expressed in surprising ways. All of these will expand your options.

If you are genuinely working at the gut level, you will notice the subtle ways that you are struggling to overcome conflicting perspectives. The more you want to protect a perspective, the more you will be personally pulled into a situation or thrown out of it. Getting a confirmation that we are protected strongly supports our sense of integrity; the more confirmed we feel, the more we are drawn to the power of feeling good and the pull of our selected self-image.

Keep in mind: everything we pre-decide plays into the default logic we use. How are you organizing the evidence? Does that organization shift your appreciation for either risk or opportunity? Might that be limiting you?

For example, suppose you had an upsetting fight with your spouse yesterday about chores. Today, despite your having done the chores, your spouse is now taking issue with your parents' upcoming visit. Your default utility might make it seem that raising the subject of the chores would be an opportunity (it would very confirming). But another part of you understands that the two issues are separate (which is not so confirming). If you take the Middle Path, might that rush for protection be reduced?

Appetite and spirit are the inner complements to a life well lived. If you are working at a gut level, what appetite wants is concrete confirmation. In this case, the outcome is the preferred result that brings you to a new place. In contrast, what spirit wants is a fulfilling relationship with deepening trust. Here, the enhanced relation is the preferred result that brings you to a new place.

When indecision creates tension, appetite and spirit are looking for resolution in contradictory ways. Is there a person, event or memory you are avoiding that feels like an obstacle just because it feels unresolved and awkward? Identify that obstacle. Alternatively, if you feel pressured by unacknowledged limitations, see if you can re-focus your attention by looking for opportunities instead.

Consider this second example. Suppose you feel ignored by your spouse. Then your spouse arrives with a list of home improvements and asks for your input. You are indecisive because you want some recognition for feeling left out, but now that she has this list, it seems like you and your input are being valued. The contradiction is feeling two things at the same time and not knowing how to resolve that. Appetite wants a concrete confirmation. Spirit wants a fulfilling relationship and a deepening of trust. If you give your attention to opportunity, then it might be possible to get some of both. You disclose that you have felt ignored and misunderstood and you confirm that the home improvement list signals how valued you are. Then you put out a request: "How about letting me talk more about what is making it hard for me to discuss this list of home improvements?"

"Better fighting" is respectful communication. Underneath most fights, there is unacknowledged ambivalence. You really wanted to make two decisions at the same time.

When thoughtful contemplation is done cooperatively, it may prompt a shift in your willingness to take action. If so, you will feel the ease and confidence you need to move forward. If not, you have slowed down your approach, so you are bringing forward new resources. If you still don't know what to do, then hold all the information you have *lightly* and try putting your attention in a new place. You may need the resource of Impersonal Agency and the skill of Direct Investigation. That is the subject of the next chapter.

Conclusion

Personal Agency depends on our evaluation of duration, scope and preference. Organizing your approach to decision making is best developed along the midpoint of the Utility Pendulum.

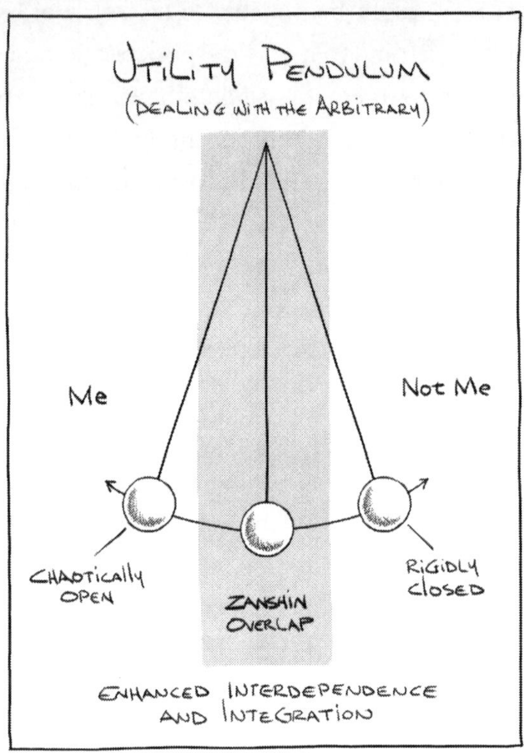

With enhanced interdependence and integration, it is not about winners and losers; it's about building a common ground that offers more for everyone. No one is given full credit and full license to decide as they want, and if we can acknowledge one another more fully, that doesn't represent much of a loss. To be zanshin is to be aware of your current circumstance and uncommitted to an outcome. The surprise, then, is the result that you never expected. (Think about Bassam who planted the dates; he never expected anything in return.)

Self-Help: Personal Agency

This chapter offered several insights that may help you when you are over-protecting in your way of seeing the world.

Directions: To complete the following, identify a problem situation that felt personally threatening, then see if the topics introduced in this chapter help you evaluate your situation differently.

Identify your problem situation here:

____

____

1. Unquestioning Feeling

How likely is it that you were under pressure from feelings you could not question or even identify?

Likely	**Not Likely**	**Unsure**
☐	☐	☐

2. Rigidity of Habits

How likely is it that you were exaggerating the situation based on a particular habit you wanted to maintain?

Likely	**Not Likely**	**Unsure**
☐	☐	☐

3. Opinions and Judgements

How likely is it that your need to be right forced you to exaggerate or distort your way of seeing?

Likely	**Not Likely**	**Unsure**
☐	☐	☐

4. Greater Awareness

How likely is it that you could be *open-endedly* committed to what you wanted, even in the face of other people's resistance?

Likely	**Not Likely**	**Unsure**
☐	☐	☐

5. The Pressure of Appetite

How likely is it that you were protecting a result you could not let go of?

Likely	**Not Likely**	**Unsure**
☐	☐	☐

6. Our Connection to Spirit

How likely is it that you wanted to trust others once they offered you something unexpected or new?

Likely	**Not Likely**	**Unsure**
☐	☐	☐

7. Working at the Gut Level

If you did *not* give in to fear and guilt, holding back, or unproductive lying, and instead used more creativity, would that be useful to you?

Likely	**Not Likely**	**Unsure**
☐	☐	☐

CHAPTER 4:

Impersonal Agency

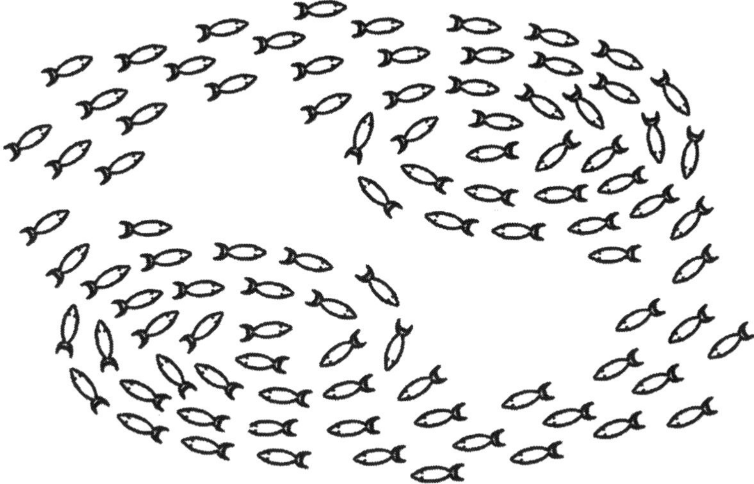

Fish don't know what they are swimming "in" but they sure know where they are going.

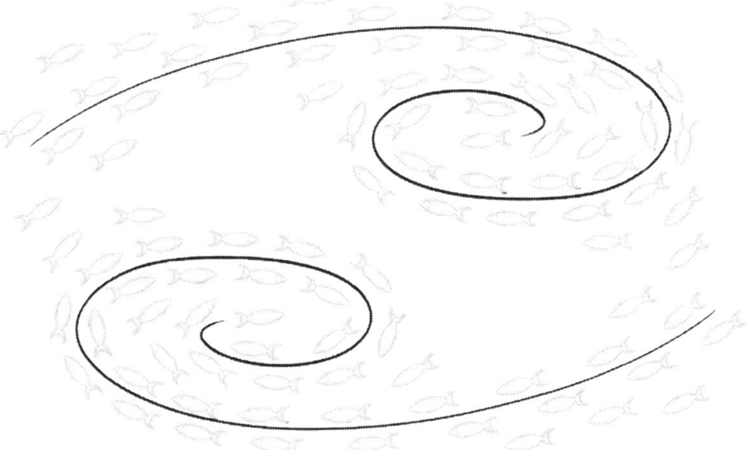

Currents don't know who's riding with them but they sure know where they are going.

CHAPTER 4:
Impersonal Agency

Duration, scope and preference are with us constantly. We use them to focus both Personal Agency and Impersonal Agency. However, given our way of pre-deciding, it's hard to tell when we are shifting from one agency to the other. If you are focused on protecting, then most likely you are still in Personal Agency. If you have shifted to discerning, then you are moving in the direction of Impersonal Agency.

Take for example the two schools of fish just illustrated. Each school thinks they have made an accurate evaluation of what they want (even though they are going in very different directions). What they might not be aware of is how the currents have taken over. Perhaps with a bit more impersonal discernment, the fish might know about that.

With Impersonal Agency, the question we must ask is: "Do I accept that what I am swimming in is driving my desire? Or do I change my way of looking at how I'm being driven along?" Which approach offers love without constraint? The more I cling to duration, scope and preference, the more likely it is that I will become either fearful at what might be taken away or euphoric at what might be offered directly and specifically to me.

Impersonal Trends

Impersonal trends are hard to support.

Impersonal Agency is the opposite of Personal Agency. With Personal Agency, you begin with reason, logic, appetite and spirit. With Impersonal Agency, you try NOT to formulate opinions and judgements using of any of these. To our normal way of thinking, Impersonal Agency is neutral and impartial, and for most of us, that feels *less* trustworthy, not more. Like the unyielding driver (who yelled "Not on your life!!!"), when we are in a conspiracy to prove what we want, the data just doesn't matter. With full credit and full license, it is tempting to believe that even impersonal information is about controlling others. We want a future that confirms our good feeling, self-image and confidence. Discernment requires not only that we stop protecting our way of thinking, but also that we change how the gut rules the measure. That's why impersonal trends are so hard to support. You must become more zanshin.

Making the Shift

Impersonal Agency is about suspending your need to be specifically directive and goal focused. Rather than trying to achieve anything, you are trying to engage with **enthusiasm**, **curiosity**, **empathy** and **imagination** for their sake, and not because they can take you anywhere. With Impersonal Agency, you are going on a quest to better understand the relation you are having without really trying to shape that relation in any specific way.

Enthusiasm, curiosity, empathy and imagination are skills that help you make the transition from a highly personal approach to a more impersonal one.

With so many arbitrary factors, these skills help you cultivate a hands-off approach. That means we must be "non-directive" and "non-driven." We may desperately want to control people, resources, schedules, and environments because they impact us so personally and directly, however, all of these impersonal factors operate, at least to some degree, like a metaphorical **black box**—everything inside the box is completely undetermined. The more we try to push a specific result through the black box, by being either directive or goal-driven, the more we force ourselves out onto the ME | NOT ME extremes that cause us to be personally involved.

When we do that, we're confirming—for our benefit and no one else's—the belief that our unique reason, logic, appetite and spirit can control whatever happens. Enthusiasm, curiosity, empathy and imagination become harder to access whenever you try and push a specific result through the impersonal black box because then you are attached to a specific result. Consequently, you learn almost nothing about the relation you are having.

Hands-off!

I tell you, there will be no rebellion

Most conspiracy theorists are prone to see "if-then" scenarios that make life more threatening than necessary. The rebellion we fear always seems to be just around the corner.

The hands-off approach of Impersonal Agency is difficult to adopt, especially when everyone else has their opinions and judgements shaped by personal experience or by a historical tradition that creates a preemptive, cultural default. The insurrection that we fear is the loss of the good feeling and confidence that comes with such a personal approach *and* that's why the other two skills of Impersonal Agency (processing feedback and negotiating the unknown) can be so very important.

Processing feedback is simply listening to whatever happens. You build a relation to feedback using the same hands-off approach that was already described as "non-directive" and "not driven." Feedback is highly charged only because it can seem so arbitrary. If we clarify how we want to *be with that first*, then we will get a lot more out of it. Being with that information from the perspective of enthusiasm, curiosity, empathy and imagination can give us a lot more information and often generates a great deal of interpersonal good will, so, most of the time, this impersonal approach creates a win-win situation for everyone.

In contrast, negotiating the unknown is about the frustration of the black box itself and our inability to know beforehand where it may be taking us. The more we look to historical precedent for guidance, the more we make the unknown predictable and concrete and that may become a limitation. Too much foresight about the black box will limit our ability to remain neutral and open.

Processing feedback and negotiating the unknown when approached *impersonally* can minimize the ME | NOT ME extremes by making it less likely that you will respond personally, reactively or even automatically, by default.

Reinforcing the SAFE Space of Being Zanshin

Well, it's back to the old drawing board.

One of the benefits of the black box is how it teaches us to start over. If we reinforce the SAFE space of being zanshin, that becomes easier.

To be zanshin is to be Stable, Adaptive, Flexible, and Energized (SAFE)—which you will not find at the Pendulum extremes. With so much built-in expectation created by the opinions and judgements of others, it is hard to make use of enthusiasm, curiosity, empathy and imagination for their own sake. But that is exactly what Impersonal Agency requires. How else would you develop your own awareness about the relation you are having, if starting over wasn't important?

Here is an old parable that illustrates how hard it is to adopt a hands-off approach and how frequently we may have to start over.

The Man, the Boy and the Donkey

A man and his son were once going with their donkey to market. As they were walking along with the donkey by their side, a countryman passed them and said, "You fools, what is a donkey for but to ride upon?"

So the man put the boy on the donkey and they went on their way. But soon they passed a group of men, one of whom said, "See that lazy youngster; he lets his father walk while he rides."

So the man ordered his boy to get off and got on the donkey himself. But they hadn't gone far when they passed two women, one of whom said to the other, "Shame on that lazy lout to let his poor little son trudge along."

Well, the man didn't know what to do, but at last he took his boy up before him on the donkey. By this time, they had come to the town, and the passersby began to jeer and point at them. The man stopped and asked what they were scoffing at. The men said, "Aren't you ashamed of yourself for overloading that poor donkey of yours—you and your hulking son?"

The man and boy got off and tried to think what to do. They thought and they thought, till at last they cut down a pole, tied the donkey's feet to it, and raised the pole and the donkey to their shoulders. They went along amid the laughter of all who met them till they came to Market Bridge, where the donkey, getting one of his feet loose, kicked out and caused the boy to drop his end of the pole. In the struggle, the donkey fell over the bridge and his forefeet being tied together, he was drowned.

"That will teach you," said an old man who had followed them: "PLEASE ALL—AND YOU WILL PLEASE NONE." [15]

This story needs little comment, but notice how Personal Agency led the man and boy to try every possible combination. Starting over is often about the outcome we are looking for, not the relation we are having.

> **Zanshin Observation:** The more you are focused on pleasing others, the less zanshin you will be. If you are hands-off, you will be engaged with every result, not just the one you already have in mind.

Enthusiasm, Curiosity, Empathy and Imagination

Why Harriet, I hardly recognized you!

Enthusiasm, curiosity, empathy and imagination are uniquely impersonal skills—and fun as well. The personal isn't supposed to be

15 This is an Aesop fable that has been carried forward for generations.

impersonal, which is why we are surprised by the newness of what we see around us. Learning about the relationship we are having pokes fun at the relationship we are having. Nothing looks the same once we shift the context of our attention.

So how do we define each of these impersonal skills?

- **Enthusiasm**—The buoyant energy we direct towards the relation we are having. Nothing happens without enthusiasm. With enthusiasm, we take on our biggest problems by supporting the relation we are having.
- **Curiosity**—Your most basic survival skill. The more curious you are, the more you will explore and learn from your environment. Your relation will change once you decide to add curiosity.
- **Empathy**—The ability to enter into and experience the world through other people's feelings. You will never learn how to be "other," even to yourself, if you fail to have empathy.
- **Imagination**—The ability to alter, change or distort your world of remembered experience. Imagination allows you to put together unrelated experiences; a blessed gift that sometimes "drives us straight to hell just so we can turn around and find heaven." This wonderful skill opens the door to all of our relations.[16]

The key to acknowledging Impersonal Agency is to accept that the black box will stay *a black box.* Bringing forward enthusiasm, curiosity, empathy and imagination requires that you disengage from imposing a preference or an outcome. All of these can limit any new information. Your enthusiasm must be both permanent and temporary. Constrain it, and your discovery becomes less effective. Equally, your enthusiasm must also be pervasive (towards everything) and

---

16 Identification of the impersonal characteristics of enthusiasm, curiosity, empathy, imagination, and processing feedback are attributed to Nicholas Boothman. He called these our human SUPERPOWERS. His description can be found online at: httpv://www.youtube.com/watch?v=HNSHvIv6AZk

blank (about nothing). One small feature and one annoying impact can become a commanding point of fascination. The same is true for curiosity, empathy and imagination. The openness of our approach and the way it includes the widest possible engagement is necessary for the discovery of new information. Amateur scientists during the Enlightenment period transformed the world with their enthusiasm curiosity, empathy and imagination.

The more you develop a hands-off approach by putting aside any preferences or outcomes, the more you will get out of each skill. Enthusiasm, curiosity, empathy and imagination are paintbrushes that we open-endedly use to understand the relation we are having.

And-So, the Magic Painter

Once upon a time, there was a poor orphan boy named And-So, who lived in a small village out in the foothills of China. He earned his living by working as a laborer. In his spare time, he would sit under the shade of a huge teak tree and draw pictures with the sticks he found there. He drew pictures of the mountains, rivers and people that looked very life-like. And-So did not have any money to buy a fancy, expensive paintbrush, but people who saw his paintings were filled with wonder and appreciation.

Soon his fame as a painter grew. One day while working at a farm, And-So felt very tired and though it was only afternoon, he fell asleep. In his dream he met a fairy princess, the native spirit of the teak tree. The fairy princess spoke to him and said, "And-So, people appreciate your painting talent; therefore, I want to give you this paintbrush. Use it any way you want." The fairy princess then put a golden brush next to the boy and vanished.

When And-So got up from his sleep, he found a golden brush lying next to him. To test the magic of his dream, And-So painted a plate and filled it with fish, shrimp, rice and fruits—everything he wanted to eat. To his surprise, the plate and food magically turned real. And-So was delighted and ate the food with great relish. He then painted a set of new clothes—an outfit for a traditional laborer. Lo and behold, these, too, became real. And-So took off his torn and worn out clothes and put on his fresh, new ones.

The next day, And-So went to the village and gathered all the poor people. With his golden brush, he painted food—hot steaming rice, fish curry and all kinds of fruits—and he fed the people the food of his imagination. The people blessed him and wished him great happiness. The fairy princess was pleased. And-So stayed very close to the huge teak tree, for there his imagination and painting seemed to flourish and grow. And-So wondered why he had been so blessed. He decided his blessings were due to his imagination, curiosity, enthusiasm and his empathy for others. And-So's magic was a benefit to others, and this made him happy.

And-so *on*, and so *on*, and so *on*—happiness found its way among the many.[17]

Impersonal Agency is a great equalizer. By opening a door to the black box and by not imposing a preference or outcome, enthusiasm, curiosity, empathy and imagination can offer love an open-ended invitation. Yes—love. For what else is both permanent and temporary, both pervasive and limited, and both preferentially worthy and preferentially true (the three markers of a decision-making preference), other than the relation we discover without knowing anything beforehand?

If the world is ever-flowing from indeterminacy, then any shift in the way that we perceive that indeterminacy will change the way we relate to one another. By imagining different futures, the world we live in changes with us, and so too, does our relation to one another.

17 (Modified). Based on the story, "The Magic Paintbrush." See http://www.worldstories.org.uk/stories/story/154-the-magic-paint-brush and the YouTube variation at https://www.youtube.com/watch?v=7u8vYYBCEA0

The world that flowed from And-So and his paintbrush is the mental creation that organizes our relation. The point is to not let it become personal or make too many pre-decisions.

Zanshin Observation: Enthusiasm, curiosity, empathy and imagination are part of the black box of indeterminacy. You will not be zanshin if they illustrate only one thing. Use them to illustrate a changeable relation—not a fixed one.

Unwinding Our Vulnerability: Achievement, Acceptance and Control

Look at it this way, *you're* the baby cardinal and *I'm* the mamma cardinal.

Change can feel maddeningly overwhelming. Vulnerability makes it twice as hard to trust the impersonal nature of how things turn out.

To enter more fully into the Impersonal Agency, you must recast the way you defend your vulnerabilities. The more you are drawn into the arbitrariness of adversity, the more you will use old habits and tricks without really thinking.

In the illustration above, it's *not* that the paratrooper doesn't want to fulfill his duty; it's just that he doesn't have any experience. Confidence draws energy from the good feeling and self-image we have, so a hands-off approach that can trust "the impersonal way that things turn out" requires us to unwind the vulnerability created by every past memory of achievement, acceptance and control—or, in this case, the paratrooper's lack of all three.

Achievement, Acceptance and Control are ways of orienting to the world that create hot-button issues, which confound and impede our efforts to get along. Those oriented toward *achievement* cannot fail. Those oriented toward *acceptance* cannot be ignored or unloved. Those oriented toward *control* must be in charge. These terms that indicate unconscious sources of vulnerability originated from Reivich and Shatte's book, *The Resilience Factor*.

Part of the arbitrariness of adversity is how events are sewn into time. The present extends itself into the future and foreshadows the hope that nothing *could* change or the fear that nothing unexpected *might* happen. The present is how the future *will go* if everything is left alone. Like the story of the man and the boy pulling the donkey, we often want to start over by pleasing those who can help create change, never realizing that we possess that power ourselves if we can release the vulnerability we feel. The pre-decision that commands our attention is how easily we are swayed by any lack of agreement.

This arbitrariness underscores much of our social vulnerability.

Another part of adversity's arbitrariness is how we judge *others* will respond. Will they support our understanding or not? Participating with Impersonal Agency by letting go of prior commitments that require us to understand and see the world in a specific way *is hard,* and it is also *necessary* if we are to improve our decision-making power.

Achievement, Acceptance and Control define that which is *most personal* to us and they represent barriers that make it hard to be satisfied with the hands-off approach required by Impersonal Agency.

Let's look at each one of these and see how we might unwind the vulnerability associated with each.

Achievement

Achievement is about embracing the virtues of personal success; however, without moderation, the discernment which Impersonal Agency generates can be too threatening to those who merely want more of the same.

Those oriented toward achievement have a fear of failure. They are compelled to measure the world as a battle between winners and losers. The vulnerability they feel makes every decision a critical test of individuality and independence. There is little need for sharing one's time and talent with others if those efforts do not yield a personal result that correlates with the virtue of success.

When we are more impersonally connected, we share our time and talents without creating a need for fame, recognition, status or "pay back." So unwinding the vulnerability of achievement means discerning that we are good enough. The insecurity of too much variability (which discernment can lead to) makes the use Impersonal Agency difficult.

The struggle to being good enough often shows up as a clown-like fear; we do not know how to let go of our personal way of understanding and seeing the world. We fear both the potential chaos that might ensue and the rigidity of other people's judgement.

Will My "Best" Be Good Enough?

> Matthew had only one task; but he didn't know if he was good enough to achieve it. Every time he thought about what he might do, he was torn between feelings he wanted to possess and those he wanted to run away from. If he decided "correctly," then he would find safety, peace, respect, belonging, success, bravery, confidence and happiness. If he decided "incorrectly," then he would have to redouble his efforts and run away from failure, anger, humiliation, hurt, sadness, fear, insecurity and loneliness.

> He asked his friend, "Will my best be good enough?" His friend said, "If you expect the world of yourself and achieve nothing, what happens then? Can you live with that?"
>
> Matthew thought about it and said, "It's not the result I want, but the feeling that I participated and tried. That, to me, is the most important." [18]

To gain strength from Impersonal Agency, Matthew had to unwind his vulnerability. By being okay with whatever happened, he made himself good enough for the task at hand. Being able to do that was his first step towards a better and more open-ended use of enthusiasm, curiosity, empathy and imagination.

Consider the earlier illustration of the paratrooper. If we take a leap of faith, deciding beforehand that our best will be good enough that might still leave us worried and afraid, but then we can take in the fellowship and support that is there already. That's one of the prerequisites for courage. You have to decide that your best really is good enough.

> **Zanshin Observation:** You are good enough! You will have a hard time using Impersonal Agency if you cannot feel that INSIDE yourself. All the skills of Impersonal Agency expand once you decide you are "good enough."

Acceptance

Acceptance is about finding comfort in the adoration of others. Without moderation, the discernment which Impersonal Agency generates can feel threatening especially when specific kinds of attention are denied to us. Adoration requires too much.

Those oriented toward acceptance are afraid of being ignored or unloved. From the side of Personal Agency, the energy of acceptance

18 This short piece is based on my imagination. There is no direct source.

and the vulnerability it creates can be so great that people often feel as if they will lose themselves if the world cannot accept them just as they understand themselves.

When we *suffer* great difficulties, we often discover positive feelings that unexpectedly come out of the difficulties we face. From the Impersonal side, these positive feelings are the genuine supports we need to discern the Middle Path. Only when we find ourselves at peace are we able to experience life more fully. Even so, acceptance must be guided by discernment—learning how to tell the difference between what we can change and what we cannot. The Impersonal challenge we face is learning to accept everything that happens.

Don't Give up Your Goodness

A man saw a bug floundering around in the water. He decided to save it by stretching out his finger, but the bug stung him. The man still tried to get the bug out of the water, but it stung him again. On seeing this, his friend told him to stop trying to save the bug that kept stinging him. But the man said, "It is the nature of the bug to sting. It is my nature to love. Why should I give up my nature to love just because it's the bug's nature sting?[19]

To unwind the vulnerability created by wanting acceptance, we must find an even deeper place of acceptance. The more we are drawn to that awareness without being overly committed to any one action or decision, the more we can access and use the enthusiasm, curiosity, empathy and imagination. Incomprehensible acceptance is nature's predecision.

> **Zanshin Observation:** To be zanshin is to accept whatever happens. If you accept the world, then the world can accept you.

19 (Not modified). This traditional scorpion story has many versions. See http://www.wisdomcommons.org/virtue/1-acceptance/parables

Control

Control is about forcing the world to conform to your expectation. Control often feels very "matter of fact." If we objectively understand the world then, of course, it will follow the rules and laws that we recognize. But then, nothing would seem arbitrary, now would it?

Those oriented toward control always desire to be in charge. If the world behaves in a capricious way, this desire for control can become so strong that people often presume that the world will overrun them entirely if it does not behave in *their* expected way.

When expectations are challenged, we can either retreat into a world of our own making or we can surpass that urge by being open to whatever happens. Only by surpassing expectation do we adapt and discover the satisfaction of our being "other," even to ourselves. However, that being said, control must be guided by discernment—by learning how to distinguish between the "shoulds," "oughts" and "musts" that shape the mechanics of control. The rules and laws we create for one another can be harder to figure out than those devised by nature.

Should-Ought-Must

We face a crossroad every day—what do we do with should, ought and must?

Should is about others. When we think "should," we are allowing ourselves to be controlled by others.

Ought is for a larger purpose. We may or may not participate in that purpose, or we may have forgotten what that larger purpose might be; however, "ought" tries to compel agreement based on some larger wish for anticipated fulfillment.

Must is entirely "for" us. We cannot let ourselves be so controlling that our "must" becomes a "should" to others.

Now, consider: When you decide to look for your dreams out there in the real world, where do you go? The crossroad of control looks different once the fulfillment we seek lives inside—not outside.

Take for an example, Susan. She was at the crossroad: to marry Mark—or not? Consider these two alternatives which she (or anyone) might use to evaluate a decision:

- If we are controlling, everything becomes a should, ought or must. We are most satisfied when the world meets our expectations.
- If we are open-endedly pursuing our dreams, there will be no should, ought or must; that's because we are learning how we fit into our dreams—and not the other way around.

Susan, in her decision, is pursuing a dream, so her need for fulfillment is different than her everyday decisions.

If that distinction feels awkward to you (that is, how can a dream be similar to or different from an everyday decision), consider this way of identifying when we are pursuing a dream rather than just making a decision.

A *job* is done for money, 9:00–5:00 and out; we are committed to a narrowly defined result.

A *career* is done for advancement and promotion; we are committed to a purpose.

A *calling* is intrinsically fulfilling; we "must" live its truth into every day because it is integral to the dream that we carry inside with no prompting or promoting.

Susan decided to marry Mark. Why? Because a calling is a must that never becomes a should to anyone else. Now, Susan can participate with enthusiasm, curiosity, empathy and imagination and never be constrained by the possible expectations that might limit her decisions. That open-ended giving is, of course, the essence of what a marriage "ought" to be, if we haven't forgotten the purpose of marriage![20]

---

20 Loosely based on two sources: https://medium.com/@elleluna/the-crossroads-of-should-and-must-90c75eb7c5b0#.adef31g0j, and the TED talk that was cited in the blog. http://www.ted.com/talks/stefan_sagmeister_the_power_of_time_off#

To unwind the vulnerability created by control, we must embrace a calling. Not everything we do will move us toward some vision or dream, so some level of control is a necessary by-product that asks a little bit from everyone. There is no coordination *without control.* However, whenever we use our expectations to control others, we are using Personal Agency to get exactly what we want. The more open-ended we are in how we manage our need for control, the more we can access and use enthusiasm, curiosity, empathy and imagination in a way that is larger than any ONE preconceived expectation.

This unwinding, however, is more a "feeling" than a "reason," which is why the black box of indeterminacy can be so difficult. By approaching our feelings more open-endedly, we are fitting our lives into our dreams, and not the other way around. Impersonal Agency draws upon that which is permanent and temporary (in duration), pervasive and limited (in scope), and preferentially worthy and true (in its "feeling" of preference)—but in a way that is altogether different from Personal Agency. If we want to coordinate with others based on impersonal facts, then we ought to be in the center of the pendulum swing: situationally *aware* but *uncommitted* to any result that personalizes who we are or what we are about.

Zanshin Observation: The dream is larger than one result or purpose. By living into the vision of your calling, you can become zanshin. Be large enough to accept that.

The gift of interdependence is accepting the idea that others *do have a role to play.* The clown who ignores (or denies) that idea by exaggerating his need for Achievement, Acceptance, and Control, will wind up tripping over *our* feet.

The personal is "I am *that* **I am.** Nothing else matters." The impersonal is "**I am** because there is *'other.'* Only evidence matters." If by adopting the latter point of view can we discern how others are behaving toward us, then we must do so without letting go of the former. Protection has its place, but so too does discernment.

Uncertain Clouds of Vagueness

Perhaps there is a simple explanation.

The playfulness of enthusiasm, curiosity, empathy and imagination often runs up against a desire to "fix" other people. The simplest explanation for this is to acknowledge how easily we refuse the role that others play.

One might claim it is all well and good to be hands-off when possible, but with so much uncertainty at work in the world today, we cannot be hands-off all the time. Another way to say this is to claim that there are perpetual clouds of vagueness that require action—not investigation—and to a degree, that is a realistic perspective.

Nobel Laureate Kenneth Arrow highlights our willingness to accept uncertainty by accepting information as "certain" simply by belief. Most people overestimate the amount of information that is available to them when evaluating unknown risks. This tendency goes by a variety of names.

- One is the *Confirmation Bias,* our tendency to seek confirming evidence and to ignore or reinterpret disconfirming evidence.
- Another is the *Hindsight Bias,* our tendency to reconstruct the past based on what we learn after the fact.

- Still another is the *Self-Justification Bias,* our tendency to rationalize decisions after the fact just to prove that we did the right thing.
- And finally, the *Bias Blind Spot,* our tendency to be persuaded by the importance of our most urgent preferences.

Arrow's concern about certainty is that our brains will convince us we are always right. As a result, we underestimate the consequences that might potentially follow. To quote Arrow:

> …[O]ur knowledge of the way things work, in society or in nature, comes trailing clouds of vagueness. Vast ills have followed a belief in certainty, whether historical inevitability, grand diplomatic designs, or extreme views on economic policy. When developing policy with wide effects for an individual or society, caution is needed because we cannot predict the consequences…[21]

So while perhaps it is true that we cannot know everything about a choice or decision, it is also true that we must be careful. The black box of indeterminacy is not altogether inconvenient or "evil." It simply requires us to depend on one another. The benefit of Impersonal Agency is that *we can choose* to be open-minded and take the Middle Path.

Arrow argues that we play fast with certainty when, according to our evaluation, *potential losses are small while the benefits are large.* The probabilities that we judge with regard to both duration and scope are, more often than not, fitted to our preferences, which feels both reasonable and prudent. However, *what we are forecasting* is the probability of outcome, not the relationship we are having *with others.*

When we support a conviction of certainty, by belief, there is little need to consult others, especially if we are giving ourselves full

---

21 Peter L. Bernstein, *Against the Gods: The Remarkable Story of Risk*, excerpted passage on p. 203 sourced to Kenneth Arrow from a 1992 publication, "I Know a Hawk From a Handshake," pg. 46.

credit and full license to do as we want. Impersonal Agency offers us a way to engage in the necessary conversations that can prevent the unexpected losses that might otherwise happen if we play fast with any pre-decided conviction.

Along the same lines, certainty often convinces us that the simplest route is the most prudent one. Here too, Impersonal Agency allows for greater engagement by requiring more substantive communication than Personal Agency.

In the face of billowing clouds of vagueness, we imagine that things are clearer than they are. The cognitive biases outlined above serve to build up and feed into the good feeling, self-image and confidence we already have. Never mind the contributions and talents of others.

Because the protection generated by Personal Agency often has no justification other than convenience and comfort, frustration will be a natural by-product of Impersonal Agency unless we are willing to use the six skills that keep us on the Middle Path, but the benefits of doing so are potent and real.

Take for example how frustration can benefit us by forcing us to slow down and uncover information we missed. Even the smallest frustration prompts a reexamination. Necessity is the mother of invention purely because Personal Agency cannot assert what it wants. The more frustrating the situation, the more resourceful we become. We attune and notice more by tolerating frustration and by temporarily setting aside the vulnerability we feel. That's why Achievement, Acceptance and Control can impede cooperation, they prevent us from adopting the "hand-off" stance which Impersonal Agency requires.

The take-away here is that no matter how daunting it is to work through feelings of frustration, if you are too certain about your process and about the outcomes you are looking for, you will discover very little that is new. The more you activate some engagement with Impersonal Agency, the less you will be blindsided by assumptions you unconsciously make, especially about others.

It all comes back to how easily we refuse the role that others play. Here is a short story to illustrate that.

Elephant and the Blind Men

A long time ago, there lived six blind men in a village who had never seen an elephant.

Each one was curious, so together they decided to see what they might learn simply by touching one part of the elephant.

"The elephant is like a pillar," said the first man who touched his leg.

"Oh, no! It is like a rope," said the second man who touched the tail.

"Oh, no! It is like a thick branch of a tree," said the third man who touched the trunk of the elephant.

"It is like a big hand fan," said the fourth man who touched the ear of the elephant.

"It is like a huge wall," said the fifth man who touched the belly of the elephant.

"It is like a solid pipe," said the sixth man who touched the tusk of the elephant.

They all began to argue about the elephant and every one of them insisted that he was right.

A wise man passed by and upon seeing this he asked, "What is the matter?"

They said, "We cannot agree as to what an elephant is like." Each one of them told what he had experienced. The wise man calmly explained, "All of you are right. The reason every one of you has a different conclusion is that you are generalizing from too small an observation."

"Oh," everyone said. "But how can all of us be right?" asked one of the blind men.

> The wise man answered, "You've been led to believe in your own preferences because that is what you experienced. A partial experience is not a complete experience. Each of you has more to learn, and still more importantly, more to experience. But you will always be larger if you share your experiences with others."[22]

The black box of indeterminacy can only generate a partial picture, so we must depend on one another to enlarge our understanding. Impersonal Agency allows us to do that by developing enthusiasm, curiosity, empathy and imagination so we can share our experiences with others. We don't want to refuse the role that others play.

> **Zanshin Observation:** Frustration can be useful. To be zanshin is to discover how the remaining mind already knows this and uses it to shape a more complete relationship with others.

Processing Feedback

What gets me is why they made all their buildings look like banks.

22 (Lightly modified). Based on the traditional Jainist story, "Elephant and the Blind Men." See http://www.jainworld.com/literature/story25.htm.

Processing feedback can have a degree of circularity, if we only reference our point of view. Like the couple here, the "selfie" we take builds on everything we already know. The challenge is to be open enough so we can step outside the confines of that, especially when pressured by others.

To be zanshin is to be Stable, Adaptive, Flexible, and Energized (SAFE)—which you cannot find at the ME | NOT ME extremes. Processing feedback challenges your being SAFE. With so much self-generated expectation coming from experience, it is hard to make use of enthusiasm, curiosity, empathy and imagination with flexible openness. We are unconsciously inclined to show enthusiasm for what is most familiar to us, be curious about certainties that preoccupy us, be more empathetic towards perspectives that command our attention, and use imagination to reinforce the good feeling, self-image and confidence we *already* have. Like the frustration needed for discovery, a little bit of friction helps us to move past the circularity of our own point of view.

Processing feedback is difficult because so often we choose to take it personally. The more we listen and see feedback as a contrast to the reason, logic, appetite, and spirit we use, the more we fear that we *must* reject ourselves. Feedback offends and challenges us in ways that make it hard to sustain relationship, leading to alienation and separation.

Processing feedback reinforces our perception *of* and belief *in* learned helplessness. If we cannot trust ourselves, then none of our decisions will make sense, nor will they "make more" by "doing better."

Learned helplessness is a feeling of powerlessness, arising from a repeated trauma that has instilled a persistent belief in one's own inability to succeed. With enough adverse repetition, we cease to feel capable and we no longer try.

Let me give you an example: Elephant trainers chain baby elephants to large wooden pegs knowing that the frustration of being chained will eventually translate into a state of learned helplessness. After years of experience, adult elephants consistently accept the "message" of the wooden peg, even though they could easily use their natural, physical power to pull it out of the ground.

Here's another example: OPPORTUNITYISNOWHERE

If you unconsciously split the letters and read "opportunity is nowhere"—rather than "opportunity is now here"—you have a stronger association with risk than with opportunity. That's the beginning of learned helpless.

Learned helplessness is the opposite of being SAFE. When you cannot protect, you defer to fear. When you cannot discern, you defer to the unknown. When you cannot confirm, you resist by withholding trust. The more we process feedback in a *personal* way, the more we reinforce a learned relational stance that most often feels negative rather than positive.

William Glasser, in his book, *Positive Addiction*, identified the importance of creating the optimal conditions that allow our brains to grow so that they pattern together the "lessons" of experience in a positive rather than a negative way. The more we approach feedback from the impersonal side (by utilizing enthusiasm, curiosity, empathy and imagination), the more we will draw optimistic lessons that reinforce what is positive, not what is negative.

Glaser's point is that while no one chooses helplessness, they can with effort and repetition choose against helplessness. Duration, scope and preference, from the personal side, create attitudes that we would never consciously select. However, from the impersonal side, we can choose to set aside the attitudes that make it hard to succeed.

For example, famous jazz pianist Keith Jerrett was forced to perform on a keyboard that, to his judgement, was virtually unusable. When he rendered a stunning performance that surprised everyone, including himself, he generated an impossible result that no one could have predicted.[23]

The optimal condition that allows our brains to draw strength from whatever happens is a belief in an "impossible future."

23 This example describes the experience of Keith Jarrett at the Cologne Opera House. See https://en.wikipedia.org/wiki/The_K%C3%B6ln_Concert

Learning, in essence, is a survival pleasure[24] that overcomes the inertia and pain of feeling helpless. This learning is largely impersonal. We survive by choosing and re-choosing to be enabled by whatever happens—not resistant to it.

Making the shift from Personal Agency to Impersonal Agency allows us to avoid the immobilizing fear that reinforces and supports learned helplessness. The survival pleasure of an "impossible future" is greater than the contingent limits we remember when fixating on the past. Feedback is opportunity whereas the past is just another "selfie."

Another way to look at this personal-impersonal tension is to examine how attentional filters work. *Attentional filters* are filters used in the self-organization of attention based on perceived importance. Duration, scope and preference are filters that elicit remembered good feeling, self-image, and confidence. As attentional filters, they are symptomatic of emotion and unconscious motivation; however, individuals can selectively choose what they will attend to by suppressing any stimulus deemed meaningless or irrelevant.

With Personal Agency, our attentional filters are looking for contradictions. We are obsessed with being made "wrong." Protection is more important than discernment.

With Impersonal Agency, our attentional filters are open; we accept a greater variety of information. We are ready to learn. The survival pleasure of the "impossible future" is more important than security of protection.

A small amount of frustration can lead to optimal results because we must choose to be larger than our frustration. When we make this choice, we become more creative and committed to a positive orientation that willingly looks past the frustrations of the immediate

24 Survival pleasure (coined term) refers to the survival value given to neurological responses that are passed on over time. These neurological adaptations may coordinate with the collective unconscious, thereby yielding a survival pleasure that overcomes any one way of responding. Choosing against helplessness is a survival pleasure that, by example, supports many, not just a lone individual who happens to be a survivor.

moment. Difficult as it is, can we suppress our attentional filters long enough to be released from learned helplessness? Yes, and the more we can do that, the more zanshin we will become.

Here is a short story to illustrate that principle.

Botan's Three Tests

A very popular and beloved monk, Botan, lived alone on the side of a Japanese mountain. He was popular because he was considered a great sage of wisdom and he was beloved because his calling was to serve others as best he could.

Even the gods in heaven recognized his many virtues, except for one angel, who disbelieved that any human being could be so thoroughly cleansed of their need for comfort and adoration.

To test Botan, the angel disguised himself as a sick, old monk. Then, by messenger, Botan was informed that an old monk with many ailments was in need of his help. The angel knew that every monk must take a vow of servitude, which required them to assist others. This was how he would catch Botan in the weakness of being human.

Botan immediately went to the sick, old monk carrying a large jug of the purest water. The sick old monk said, "I have been wretched and suffering for a long time. You do not care if someone needs your help, nor do you try to find others to help them."

Botan was not offended by these words. He had developed virtues of tolerance, forgiveness, and compassion. He calmly replied, "Oh, best of the monks, kindly excuse my oversight. I have brought pure water for you to drink," and so the testing began.

The disguised angel's tests were threefold:

- A *physical* test. Would Botan accept hardship without complaint?

- A *spiritual* test. Would Botan find beauty in the ugliness of another who was mean-spirited?
- A *logical* test. Would Botan choose to be the same or different from the one he served?

The first test was to carry the sick, old monk up the mountainside on his shoulders, which Botan did while the disguised angel slowly increased the weight with every step. Botan never complained.

The second test was to repeatedly offer the mean-spirited old monk the benefit of spiritual beauty. No matter how degrading or insulting the old monk became, Botan accepted the beauty of the old monk's life and being. He never became spiteful or angry at the hardships the disguised angel heaped onto him.

Finally, the last test was the logical one. The old monk put to Botan the question: "I am an old, vile man, conceived to hate myself and others and to hate everything that the gods have ever created; are you the same or different from me?"

Botan said, "When washed by pure water, we are one and the same. I am no different from you; you are no different from me." Botan understood that the nature of life's journey is to be like pure water and go wherever he was needed. In that way, he was the same as everyone he served.[25]

Botan's approach to feedback was both humane and impersonal. So long as he was serving others, he did not require comfort or adoration. To have expected that would have resulted in learned helplessness, since a monk's vow of servitude must deny those benefits. Equally, Botan's attentional filters would have been focused on ugliness and hardship, and not beauty. However, to be like "pure

25 (Modified). Based loosely on the Janist story, "Sage Nandisen." See http://www.jainworld.com/literature/story10.htm. The three tests presented above are different from the source and the pointed references to "pure water" are also not found in the primary source.

water" was enough; Botan was both vessel and substance. The pleasure of his "impossible future" was more important than protecting any personalizing benefits. Botan was striving to be the same as the people he served—no different in any way.

> **Zanshin Observation:** Learned helplessness comes from personal experience. Processing feedback impersonally gives us the opportunity to be like pure water. To let go of helplessness, we must be as transparent as possible and without constraint.

Negotiating the Unknown

THAT drawing is you, I suppose.

Nothing is more difficult than being "unknown" to someone else. Like the domestic couple above, representations and the recognition they create cloud our judgement whenever we feel left out. Being skewered and cooked is how we feel when recognition is withheld.

Former president of Egypt, Anwar Al Sadat, wisely said: "He who cannot change the very fabric of his thought will never be able to change reality, and will never, therefore, make any progress."

Negotiating the unknown challenges us because it pushes aside the good feeling, self-image, and confidence we are accustomed to. The "**I am**—because there is *other*" point of view prioritizes the evidence, not feeling (even though duration, scope and preference are always based on feeling). Here, our angst is focused on opposing and denying evidence which might diminish the "I am" part of what we recognize even while focusing on evidence. Individual discernment resists the excess of being unknown even to one's self. Only the most zanshin can do this.

Consider the scientific revolutions that so confounded the good feeling, self-image, and confidence of traditional orthodoxy that they were rejected for centuries—not because evidence was lacking, but because traditional explanation could not give the evidence a status equal to accepted knowledge. The unknown, like the arbitrary, seemingly took away power because the evidence confounded the trust that assembled and made sense of available evidence. Unlike the bias blind spot that shapes personality and Personal Agency, here the bias blind spot is simply the dismissal of contrary evidence and contrary belief. Traditionalists with orthodox opinions do not know how to bring enthusiasm, curiosity, empathy and imagination to evidence that contradicts the recognition which they themselves have been asked to generate and support.

Eric Hoffer wrote, "In times of change learners inherit the earth; while the learned find themselves beautifully equipped to deal with a world that no longer exists." Scientific breakthroughs are replete with worlds that no longer exist, and yet the observing and measuring heart continues nonetheless.

Each of the scientists below offered "discoveries" that were ridiculed as "garbage science" and suppressed for a significant period of time. Only later were they vindicated by a shift in orthodox opinion.

- Crick & Watson (DNA)
- Christian Doppler (optical Doppler effect)
- Galileo (supported the Copernican viewpoint)

- Karl F. Gauss (nonEuclidean geometery)
- James Lovelock (Gaia theory)
- Barbara McClintlock ("jumping genes")
- George S. Ohm (Ohm's Law)
- Louis Pasteur (germ theory of disease)
- Max Planck (quantum-mechanics)
- Wilbur & Orville Wright (flying machines)
- George Zweig (quark theory)
- Fritz Zwicky (existence of dark matter)

Negotiating the unknown is the sixth skill of Impersonal Agency. It challenges the "set" ways we have for using and sharing support—both for ourselves and for others. Unlike our caveman ancestors, to negotiate the unknown requires us to suspend our preferential, everyday reason and logic so we might learn more about ourselves without directly acting in support of anything at all. The midpoint of the pendulum swing is the only place where we can do this.

Consider briefly the full length of life's journey: experientially, we start with nothing and end with nothing other than our capacity to love (the single motivator of Core Essence). Using what Core Essence notices, reason and logic (the duel drivers of Ego) build a pattern of thinking is preferentially determined by selectively choosing what feels "lovable." This in turn supports the good feeling, self-image and confidence we feel.

Everything that we know *now* was, originally, at one point, *unknown to us*—both as something shared or even supported by us. So, to negotiate the unknown, we must suspend any interpretation and in that vacuum, learn to draw support from our experience in a new way. Every time we do that, we are changing the way we are connected and engaged both with ourselves and others. This describes the Core Essence to Ego dialog that takes place around experience.

The question is: Can we tolerate the anxiety of being disconnected long enough to change our understanding of ourselves and others? Being skewered and cooked metaphorically is naturally a challenge.

Let's take an example. Up until the 1880's, the consensus in Europe was that swans only have white feathers. However, with the discovery of Australia, it was observed that swans do exist *with black feathers*. Every observable occurrence of a swan up until that point confirmed that swans were universally *only* white. After that **one** observation, the entire orthodoxy of what a swan could be suddenly changed. If I put forth no interpretation and open-endedly observe, I am (implicitly) open to changing my "understanding" of myself and others. Impersonal Agency allows me to do this.

However, given that our way of understanding is preferential, we are always tempted to throw out the unknown. It takes an impartial disposition to tolerate more than one way of thinking. To reassess the preferential feeling that shapes our engagement can feel threatening. Our struggle is to put our attention somewhere else and to willingly negotiate the worthiness and truthfulness of what we *might* discover—all without the benefit of *exact* knowledge.

Here is a short story that illustrates that struggle.

While Standing on One Foot

Rabbi Hillel was a first-century rabbinical scholar, well-beloved for his patience and for his surprisingly concise wisdom.

One day a student made a wager with his friends that he could make Rabbi Hillel lose his temper. He did not believe that Rabbi Hillel was as patient and as wise as everyone said.

To implement his plan, the unruly student was going to badger the rabbi until he was fed up with him. "Surely if I question him long enough, the rabbi will eventually lash out in anger," he thought.

That morning in class, the unruly student was incessant: "Rabbi, Rabbi," he cried. "Why do Babylonians have round heads?" .... "Why do the Egyptians have flat feet?" ... "Why do the Numidian people have such weak eyes?" To each of these inquiries, the rabbi remained unperturbed and patiently answered in a concise way, hoping to get back to his main topic. But this unruly student was unrelenting. He had made an exceptionally large wager and was not willing to accept the awkwardness of his situation.

Thinking fast, the unruly student hit upon the one way that he could be sure to get a rise out of Rabbi Hillel: force him to do the impossible. Seizing his chance, the unruly student stood up in front of the class and started jumping up and down on one foot, saying, "Rabbi, Rabbi! Can you teach me the whole of Torah while I stand on one foot?" Everyone stared at the young man. People spend their entire lives studying the Torah. There was no way the rabbi could answer such a question. While everyone was transfixed with apprehension, the unruly student continued hopping up and down like a stork, flapping his wings and squawking his question: "Can you teach me the whole of Torah while I stand on one foot?"

Rabbi Hillel looked calmly at the student and said, "That which is hateful unto yourself, do it not unto your neighbor. That is the whole of Torah. The rest is commentary. Now go and learn."

The unruly student became perfectly still. Then he said, "I never would have thought it possible. My bet was a sure thing! There cannot be another person like you. Now I see exactly just how stupid I've been!"

The unruly student's preferred way of thinking was upended. Without the benefit of exact knowledge, he gained new respect for his own integrity and for the integrity of others by losing that bet. What was worthy and truthful was larger than himself or the rabbi. The poetic justice of "standing on one foot" is that only by challenging the world could the unruly student learn what he needed, and as a result, everyone was changed. The impossible was not impossible.[26]

---

26 (Modified). Based on a rabbinical story by Nina Jaffe and Steve Zeitlin, *While Standing on One Foot: Puzzle Stories and Wisdom Tales from the Jewish Tradition*, Henry Holt and Company, New York, 1993, pp 91-93.

Remember this story when negotiating the unknown. Put forth no interpretation and stand on one foot! The worth and truth of what you discover will be larger than you expect.

> **Zanshin Observation:** The impossibility of the unknown is that we cannot know it. So if we want to expand what *we think* we know, we must depend on one another, not ourselves.

Indecision and Impersonal Agency

The inner and the outer realms are difficult to manage. If you see no immediate option, can you still be impartially engaged and learn something unexpected about your situation? It is one thing to discover utility from a highly personal point of view; it is another to revise that utility based on additional information and new experience.

Remember the observations that have been made in this chapter:

- The more you are focused on pleasing others, the less zanshin you will be.
- Enthusiasm, curiosity, empathy and imagination are part of the black box. Use them to illustrate a relation—not as a result.
- You are good enough! You will have a hard time using Impersonal Agency if you cannot feel that INSIDE yourself.
- To be zanshin is to accept whatever happens. If you accept the world, then the world can accept you.
- The dream is larger than one result or purpose. By living into your vision, you will become large enough to understand and accept that.
- Frustration can be useful. To be zanshin is to discover how the remaining mind already knows this and uses it to shape a more complete relationship with others.

- Learned helplessness comes from personal experience. Processing feedback impersonally gives us the opportunity to be like pure water. Be as transparent as possible and without constraint.
- The impossibility of the unknown is that we cannot know it. So if we want to expand what we *think* we know, we must depend on one another, not ourselves.

❧

If you are facing a tough decision and you still don't know what to do even after "thinking" about it for a while—what do you do?

- Consider the people, resources and consequences involved and try seeing them in a different way.
- Adopt an impartial outlook so you can explore your outer environment in a more directed way.
- Do not try to make any decision. Simply try to discover some new opportunity that you potentially might have overlooked.

Personal Action and Direct Investigation

With too much focus on risk (that is, a potential loss of good feeling, self-image, and confidence), we become blind to opportunity (a potential increase in good feeling, self-image, and confidence). With Impersonal Agency, you step out of your routine way of being by not giving much attention to your normal way of responding. This might feel a bit forced at first, but with practice, you can learn to shift into an engaged, but still impartial, way of being that can begin to feel second nature to you.

The key is to use enthusiasm, curiosity, empathy and imagination to change the way you normally respond. If you treat everything in a hand's off way with no presumptions, you can piece different opportunities together in a new way.

- **Enthusiasm** is a demonstration of care and concern.
- **Curiosity** is a demonstration of interest that looks closely, but still at a distance.
- **Empathy** is the ability to enter into and experience the world through other people's feelings by listening, reflecting and attuning oneself to others.
- **Imagination** allows you to put together unrelated experiences and create unexpected insight.

Everything we encounter is specific. The more you give energy to Direct Investigation, the more attuned you become to what is unusual and different. Here is an example to illustrate that.

Situation: Jonathan is trying to decide if it is time to get his own apartment or stay in the shared apartment with his roommates. He's considered all of the usual variables: location, cost, commute, parking, as well as the much harder to determine social cost. The idea of going solo feels right, but so too does the social benefit he derives from being around others. When Jonathan realized he could not simply "think" his way through his decision, he tried something different. By employing Impersonal Agency, he gave up trying to decide and simply made a conscious effort to notice what he liked and did not like about his current living situation. To organize this effort, he created an observation list for people, resources, and consequences. For a week, he tracked his likes and dislikes while trying to keep an open mind.

People	Resources	Consequences
Molly is interesting; I never noticed how she plays with the cat.	The kitchen is better stocked than what I might have.	All of these relationships would change; I'm mixed on that.
Jason is annoying; his music is too loud.	There's a nice living room with a TV; I'm not sure I can get a TV right away.	Jason has mentioned that he might move.
Sarah has friends who come over too often but some of them have cool things to say.	Street parking is a pain, but I'm not paying for it.	I need a solo apartment someday.
The cats are fun and I doubt that I will have one if I'm solo.	The laundromat is too far away, but the basement has great storage.	We have community dinner every Monday; I would miss that.

The end result of the observation period was that Jonathan saw his situation differently because he noticed things that he missed before: the basement and the kitchen, the cats and community dinner. The social picture mattered to him more than he had realized, so he decided to put the move aside for another year.

Some of the hardest decisions are the recurring ones: to stay or go, to stop or start, to avoid or confront. All of these decisions require information that must be evaluated with neutrality in a way that is direct, but not "removed." Jonathan's first evaluation was more abstract and theoretical; his second was more tangible and concrete.

Since we cannot forecast the future and the past is closed to our changing it, we must do all our data gathering in the present. We may desperately want to change things in the present and we may also overlook potential advantages. Think about how the present "shows up"—it is a continuous feedback loop that starts with us and reaches to the outside based on the way we interact with it. The more present we are, the more likely it is that we will discover what is useful. Adding enthusiasm, curiosity, empathy and imagination allows us to access a greater range of information, especially with a recurring decision. We don't want to be blindsided by the expectations we already have; especially when there might be appreciable differences between what is "obvious" in the abstract and what is "obvious" in the actual. For example, it's well known that the shortest distance between two points is a straight line, but that's almost never true during rush hour! Actual experience counts for a lot.

To be neutral doesn't mean we acquire experience without emotion. It simply means that our feelings remain in a fluid state and that nothing is allowed to mean anything too specifically. Yes, that might seem a bit oxymoronic—"specific information that doesn't mean anything too specifically"—but if you think about it, even the unknown, indeterminate, and unexpected may not mean anything *specific* at all. It is only when we attach an expectation to it that it becomes emotionally charged. If you don't have a duration, scope and preference in mind, you probably won't notice anything much *in great detail.* Using enthusiasm, curiosity, empathy and imagination is our way of testing things out, so we are not fooled by our own expectation. It's like that unruly student hopping up and down because he believed his bet was "a sure thing." That is, until he tested it out … and suddenly, he saw that it wasn't.

With Direct Investigation, the information you glean by testing may resolve your indecision; however, sometimes by going back and forth between Direct Investigation and Direct Contemplation, you still may not have a clear path forward. If that's the case, place the intention in front of you to be open to whatever happens. You may need the resource of Divine Agency and the skill of Direct Entreaty. That is the subject of the next chapter.

Conclusion

To turn an arbitrary NOT ME event about the past into a more acceptable ME event about the future, we must evaluate duration, scope and preference. To do that impersonally challenges our defaults and requires that we trust one another in a new way.

The lesson of Object Relations is that integration is possible. We can occupy the midpoint of the pendulum swing. However, to do that, we must learn to set aside some of the arbitrariness that we embrace. If we over-discern, we are likely to be pushed out onto the extremes of the pendulum swing. Being zanshin takes a disciplined focus that willingly can accept that the remaining mind is greater and larger than both Personal Agency and Impersonal Agency.

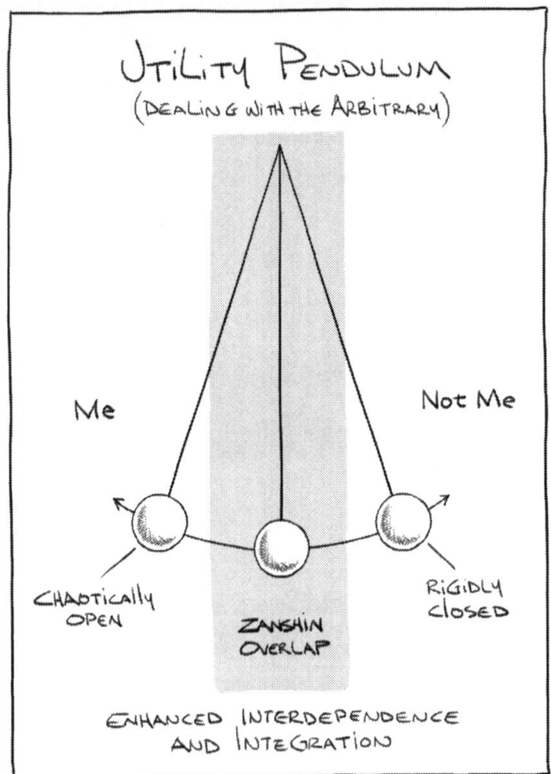

The six skills of Impersonal Agency are enthusiasm, curiosity, empathy, imagination, processing feedback and negotiating the unknown. These are the means used to realize enhanced interdependence and integration. By focusing more on these skills, you can become more zanshin. It's never that we are completely wrong or completely right in *what* we decide, it's whether we are open to being changed by making that decision, especially when we must turn to others for feedback and support.

Self-Help: Impersonal Agency

This chapter offered several insights that bring attention to how discernment might be impacting your decisions.

Directions: To complete the following, identify a situation where you had difficulty maintaining an impersonal perspective, then see if the topics introduced in this chapter help you evaluate your situation differently.

Identify your problem situation here:

____

____

1. Impersonal Trends

If your situation was impersonally determined, how likely is it that your discernment would be equally impersonal?

Likely	**Not Likely**	**Unsure**
☐	☐	☐

2. Making the Shift

If people, resources and environments are indeterminate black boxes, how likely is it that your choices would actually change?

Likely	**Not Likely**	**Unsure**
☐	☐	☐

3. Hands Off!

How likely is it that you could take a hands-off approach as you go about investigating your situation?

Likely	**Not Likely**	**Unsure**
☐	☐	☐

4. Reinforcing the SAFE Space of Being Zanshin

If being Stable, Adaptive, Flexible, and Energized (SAFE) were important to you, how likely is that you would (or more strongly) could discern more?

Likely	**Not Likely**	**Unsure**
☐	☐	☐

5. Enthusiasm, Curiosity, Empathy and Imagination

If you practiced greater use of enthusiasm, curiosity, empathy and imagination, how likely is it that a satisfying and useful solution would appear?

Likely	**Not Likely**	**Unsure**
☐	☐	☐

6. Unwinding Vulnerability: Achievement, Acceptance and Control

If achievement, acceptance and control cause you to feel vulnerable, how likely is it that you would compensate by exaggerating?

Likely	**Not Likely**	**Unsure**
☐	☐	☐

7. Uncertain Clouds of Vagueness

If certainty is impossible, how likely is it that you might forecast a conviction just to be more comfortable?

Likely	**Not Likely**	**Unsure**
☐	☐	☐

8. Processing Feedback

If feedback from others creates a barrier, how likely is it that you would use that feedback to your advantage? (Hint: Advantage would point to something larger than your immediate expectation.)

Likely	**Not Likely**	**Unsure**
☐	☐	☐

9. Negotiating the Unknown

If knowing *anything* is preferable to being in the dark, how likely is it that you could let go of your expectations?

Likely	**Not Likely**	**Unsure**
☐	☐	☐

10. Discernment as a Decision Making Need

If discerning accurately helps you to arrive at a decision, might it be useful to let go of good feeling, self-image and confidence?

Likely	**Not Likely**	**Unsure**
☐	☐	☐

CHAPTER 5:
Divine Agency
FLIGHT TRAINING
You'll never get me up in one of those!

CHAPTER 5:
Divine Agency

The difference between the story we tell ourselves and the one told to us is who is doing the telling. The two caterpillars in the preceding illustration are preoccupied *with their story*, not understanding that another story is being *told to them*. With Divine Agency, the storyteller is neither personal nor impersonal. The story is never entirely *what we make of it,* and yet unavoidably, like the caterpillars, *we are attuned to it*, cued to how the story we are being told confirms or denies the story we've been telling ourselves.

Eckardt Tolle said, "That is the real spiritual awakening, when something emerges from within you that is deeper than who you thought you were. So, the person is still there, but one could almost say that something more powerful shines through the person." Divine Agency uncovers that light because *that* is what we are working towards—provided we are willing.

Ego protects, Experience discerns, and Core Essence confirms. What Divine Agency works with most is Core Essence, the YOU who most fully is present in the Now.

The zanshin martial artist operates on the understanding that whatever unfolds will confirm his deepest longing. The remaining mind unifies what the conscious mind cannot. The result we find created and ready for us will be larger and greater than our expectation. Just like that butterfly.

Flight Training

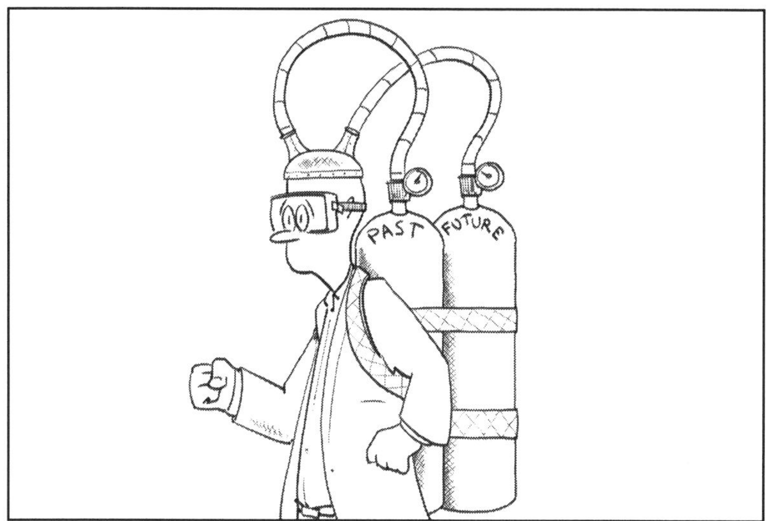

Personal Agency and Impersonal Agency are primarily products of experience, but the Flight Training of Divine Agency is found in the Now, not in any pre-packaged version of the past and future. The more we cling to the pre-decisions which those agencies create, the less we activate Core Essence.

To turn an arbitrary NOT ME event about the past into a more acceptable ME event about the future, we cannot *pre*-decide. We need only relate more fully to one another. To place our attention in the Now is not a denial of Personal or Impersonal Agency. It is a lateral shift. Drawing courage from others who focus on the Now can inspire us to do the same. Michael Jordan or Steve Jobs might be two examples. What makes an acceptable ME event is how it inspires us to excel in the ways that are unique to us. Was Michael Jordan ever constrained by a basketball? Was Steve Jobs constrained by a transistor?

As Fulton Sheen wrote, "Patience is not an absence of action; rather it is timing. It waits on the right time to act." With Divine Agency, we are contemplating time and how best to use it.

The agency we use says a lot about how we see ourselves. "I am" **not** because I am (personal), **nor even** because there is "other" (impersonal), but simply *because life itself continues* (divine). When we are patient, we understand how life continues. So when it appears that love is taken from us, it's natural to want to know "the truth" about how that happened so we can go on to love again. But more often than not, what we project is the fear that follows any withdrawal of love, not the persistence of love itself. The good feeling, self-image and confidence to which we cling feels counter-poised, ready to be taken away—not strengthened. Thus weakened, the ego counsels greater protection.

What Is 'Divine' about Divine Agency?

Divine Agency is concerned with neither outcomes nor skills; it is concerned with consent and acceptance. To focus your attention on the Now does not deny you a future. You are simply recognizing what is primary. You are parting the curtains so you can acknowledge the constancy of love that you already have. If the duration *of Now* is timeless and temporary, then love is timeless and temporary. If the scope *of Now* is pervasive and limited, then love is pervasive and limited. The primary thing you have been given is the Now. Once you consent and accept its love, everything else is secondary. When you were first loved, you acknowledged a preference and participation that was greater than anything you could fashion for yourself.

That is what makes Divine Agency divine. *The story being told* ***to us*** *is greater than the story* ***we tell ourselves****.*

Now you can deal with what is secondary with great ease. But what is secondary is still relevant and important. We cannot say, "I'm not dealing with things anymore because there is *only the Now*."[27] No. Love takes root within us, so that we can offer it back to others. We have everything we need already. The question is, are we offering that to others in a way that expands opportunities for loving, or are we protecting and discerning just to maintain what love offers us?

What we fail to appreciate is that *patience* is not an absence of action; it is a participation in the sources of potential that are greater than anything we could fashion ourselves. Any meditative practice brings a heightened quality of mindfulness that enables us to recast the narrative we hold so that our participation with love can be restored. Now, we can deal with the secondary with great ease. We are being zanshin whenever we allow mindful patience to express itself through the remaining mind and guide us back to our unique experience of love.

Divine Agency is not about a displacement or abdication of decision-making power by a supernatural being, but rather about a reconfiguration of the convictions that make any limitations significant to us in the first place. We want to know that love will return. The remaining mind offers us that promise by returning us to our preference for and participation with love—provided we are patient.

Here is a short story that illustrates this truth.

Target in the Dark

An impatient disciple was refusing to practice shooting arrows from a distance of seven feet. The master said, "Everything is

27 Eckhart Tolle, *Stillness Speaks*, New World Library and Namaste Publishing, 2003, p 52.

in the aim." But the student said, "My aim from seven feet is never going to improve if I'm never allowed to aim from greater distances."

The master said, "The aim is determined by how you approach your goal – the distance is irrelevant." To which the disciple said, "If that's true, then I should be able to hit the target blindfolded."

The master smiled. He asked the impatient disciple to meet him later that night at the outside practice range.

When the disciple arrived, the master was standing his normal distance away from the target, which meant that the target was completely hidden in the dark. There was no available light to show the master exactly where the target was.

The master settled into his firing stance, drew the bow string tight, and released the first arrow into the darkness. By sound alone, it was clear the arrow had found its target.

Then, the master immediately drew another arrow and let it fly. When the student took a light to see what had happened, the first arrow was lodged in the center of the target, while the second arrow had splintered the butt of the first one, embedding itself beside it.

The master asked, "Is it patience or skill that allows me to do this?"

The disciple said, "It is skill."

The master replied, "No. You could have skill equal to the greatest physical strength and you would not be able to do this. What your aim must have is a patience borne of a love that surrenders doubt. Then you will land the arrow where it will do the most good for everyone."[28]

---

28 (Modified). Based on *Zen in the Art of Archery* by Eugen Herrigel, Vintage Books, New York, Chapter 8, pp 79-88.

Zanshin Observation: Let your decisions come through you but not from you. The path that combines self-regard with self-discipline belongs to the remaining mind. Be pure in heart and untroubled.

Orthodoxy Is Changeable

If you picture "orthodoxy" as a fixed way of viewing an expected future, it's hard to see what allows us to change our point of view. Change makes us feel vulnerable. Like the caterpillars we saw at the start of this chapter, it's hard for us to let go of the story we have been telling ourselves.

So, what drives the orthodoxy of the stories we tell ourselves?

Consider Personal Agency. The illustration at the start of that chapter showed a ME-planet in the center of the "ME-galaxy" weeping for help and protection. The "NOT ME" planets can be threatening. The orthodoxy of what is personal here, may be too great for us to let go of. "Do I accept my current view of what is causing me pain, or do I work to change my way of seeing?" The orthodoxy of Personal Agency depends on putting your perceptions ahead of others and even ahead of the Now.

Now consider Impersonal Agency. The illustration that opened that chapter shows two schools of fish moving in different directions. The caption reads, "Fish don't know what they are swimming in, but they sure know where they are going." The fact that unacknowledged currents are driving the schools of fish apart suggests a question: "Do I accept that what I am swimming in is driving my desire, or do I change my way of looking at how I'm being driven along?" The Now is a love greater than any orthodoxy that we create. Only with Divine Agency can we actually challenge the orthodoxies that drive our perceptions.

Divine Agency is the requisite openness needed to "reset" the duration, scope and preference evaluations that dominate one's actions and behaviors. Therefore, Divine Agency is about the openness that lives "beyond" the boundaries of Personal or Impersonal Agency. With Divine Agency, we do not swim in the currents of our own desire, but rather in one another's currents. With Divine Agency we patiently and persistently learn that pain and fear can make us whole in unexpected ways, simply by sharing them more freely with others.

Alternatives to Self-Promotion

The answer to the question "How should one live?" cannot be the found in the retrenchment of established boundary patterns; it must be discovered in the ongoing generation of new patterns that change the way we choose to be. As we willingly give expression to common needs that we all share by offering help and love, Divine Agency expands our empathic and protective concerns so we can more readily join with others in common need, rather than self-promoting in opposition to or competition with one another. This shift to openness is hard to characterize other than as a 'Divine' way of living for once embraced a concord, or integrated harmony, extends the individual outward into his surroundings. Without that extension of concord, we do little more than talk past one another.

Personal and Impersonal Agency are distinct ways that we talk about ourselves and promote ourselves to others. Good feeling, self-image and confidence in storytelling indicate a level of social mastery, so we find it difficult to self-correct the personal orthodoxy of our opinions and judgements. Knowledge about evidence and how it works in the real world as impersonal orthodoxy is also difficult to self-correct. Our assessment of what we share requires an impersonal mastery that, when freely consented to, can bring us closer to one another.

The confirmation we discover with Divine Agency requires us to be open to the Now, to let it disclose to us a new way of being, and to extend without limit the concord of what we can share together. If you are zanshin with Divine Agency, the orthodoxy of your most enmeshed narratives will shift in unexpected ways. The story we self-promote to ourselves and others can change, freeing us from habits that limit us, sometimes for our entire lifetime.

The reason we resist any change of orthodoxy is the hope that springs from us when love is given power through us. The good feeling, self-image and confidence to which we cling cannot (or more strongly *will not*) be strengthened unless we find what is primary first and make the Now our friend. That requires that we set aside Personal and Impersonal Agency. We must honor and consent to what is offered in the Now: acknowledge it, accept it, and build on it. Only then, will the Zanshin Overlap change the personal and impersonal evaluations that lead us to create inflexible narratives and orthodoxies. That's why Divine Agency both *helps* and *loves* in ways we cannot understand or appreciate from a purely logical perspective. Divine Agency changes us from the inside, provided we move freely with the Now by setting aside any desire for self-promotion.

Here is a short story that illustrates this principle.

Spontaneous Identities

> The great Taoist master once dreamt that he was a butterfly fluttering here and there. In the dream, he had no awareness of his individuality as a person. He was only a butterfly. Suddenly, he awoke and found himself laying there, a person once again. But then he thought to himself, "How odd to be that which I am not: before I was a man who dreamt about being a butterfly, now I a butterfly who dreams about being a man."[29]

> **Zanshin Observation:** Nothing prepares you for freedom but freedom itself. Effortless action taken at the right time requires no self-promotion. There is only the Now.

29 (Lightly modified). Based on a traditional Zen story; see http://users.rider.edu /~suler/zenstory/zenframe.html

Moving with the Now

The benefit of moving with the Now is that it deepens trust. To take responsibility for the life we have, we must consent to the moment we are in—not so we may confirm who we have been, but rather to expand beyond those self-imposed limitations. The risk of Divine Agency is that we will settle. If the Now possesses our fullest appreciation for love—without cause or prompting—then why should we be in any way different? We might say, "All is for the best in this, the best of all possible worlds."

But there is an essential confusion here. The Now is neither the protection nor the discernment of what we self-promote. The story we are living is *not* the one we tell ourselves. To force our story into the Now confuses the Now with *what happens* in the Now. The more we maintain that confusion, the more we are imprisoned by personal and impersonal anxiety. We cannot push love into the specific forms that we create. That's why strenuously desired outcomes often feel anticlimactic. We have over-protected, over-discerned, and over-confirmed the form that love is "supposed" to take.

If we are too focused on the content of *what happens*, we will fall out of the Zanshin Overlap. We are not letting the remaining mind do its work. Unless we are genuinely aligned with the unfolding power of being zanshin, we cannot be agents of positive change. The orthodoxy of a declared "truth" will push our attention away from the Now. Only by saying "yes" without reservation can we take up the point of view that Divine Agency creates and move past the burdens and limitations of prior experience.

Take for example take the clown story introduced in Chapter 2. The "Tramp" enters the Supreme Court ready to argue the constitutionality of mandatory union payments. Watching him, we are transfixed. As arbitrary actions prevent him from deciding as he wants, it appears that all help and love have disappeared. The orthodoxy of the clown's behavior and belief has become self-defeating. As observers, we hold in secret our pain and joy at the frustration and anger for his colossal loss of good feeling, self-image and confidence. We have all been there before. To cling to an orthodoxy that leads to strained and misguided forms of anxiety or euphoria, only demonstrates an excess of self-promotion.

Perhaps no one knows the pain that this one clown feels, yet we all know exactly how limiting orthodoxy can be. Only by remaining open and laughing at ourselves can we let go of the good feeling, self-image, and confidence that encourages us to cling to orthodoxy.

While personal and impersonal orthodoxy can lead to social mastery, such mastery runs the risk of disconnecting us from others and ultimately from ourselves. The illogical nature of duration, scope and preference is that they require an "other-fulfilling" openness. We cannot promote individual (or even group) fulfillment; we must discover an "other-fulfilling" openness that brings something larger than ourselves.

For each, the revelation of Divine Agency will be different. For some, it may lead to reconciliation or forgiveness. For others, it can prompt a letting go or letting in of that which is feared or loved—or even, perhaps, a reconnection to love long forgotten or a newfound courage in oneself and one's purpose. All of these reinforce Core Essence and help us to "make more" by "doing better" with the sum total of the experience we have.

To make use of Divine Agency, we must let go of self-promotion so we may better coordinate our actions with others. Here are some examples of what can happen if we listen to Core Essence and its stronger connection to Divine Agency.

- **Reconciliation**. John betrayed his wife by having an affair. At first, he felt justified in having the affair because he was bored by his marriage. The more John began to see his wife as a genuine person (unlike the person he initially betrayed), the more able he was to reconcile with her. Divine Agency enabled John to recast the dynamic that made him feel superior to and more powerful than his wife.
- **Forgiveness**. Mary blamed Julie for taking away her job promotion. Mary felt she was entitled to the promotion and resented the preferential treatment Julie received from others. Mary eventually felt too great a burden every time she saw Julie. All those deep feelings of mistrust had to be changed. Divine Agency enabled her to exercise forgiveness and that, in turn, allowed her to see Julie as worthy of trust, because now she, herself, is worthy of that trust as well. Mary recast the dynamic that made her feel put down by Julie's success and promotion.
- **Letting go of that which is feared or loved**. Alan feared being poor and he feared being defined by other people's judgement. To counter his fear, Alan lived in a world of "not enough." If he didn't have enough money, he also felt he didn't have enough time, or the right car, or the right home, or the right job. All of Alan's fears coalesced around his relationship with money and the judgements he feared others might make. Divine Agency enabled Alan to let go of his "not enough" fear and, as a result, he was able to enjoy the time and energy he put into *all* of his life activities, not just those associated with money. Alan recast his dynamic around money by enlarging his inner feelings of wealth.

These examples illustrate how malleable our relationship with Core Essence can be. With each example, Divine Agency is *working in our favor*. What is "divine" is the degree to which we are led to something entirely unexpected, something we cannot acknowledge beforehand.

That unexpected confirmation is the remaining mind's ability to blend the three agencies together—casually, poignantly, elegantly.

The more expansive our consent, the more the ME | NOT ME dynamic will be reshaped into a freer, more expansive trust. We learn to accept that which is larger than ourselves because the story of our lives is not really about us. It's about releasing us from the burden of being alone.

To turn an arbitrary NOT ME event about the past into a more acceptable ME event about the future, we must evaluate duration, scope and preference. The agency we use says a lot about how we see ourselves. Will we confirm what we pre-decide? Or will we allow ourselves to move into vulnerability and fear?

The lesson of Object Relations is that integration is possible. We can occupy the midpoint of the pendulum swing; however, to do that we must learn to set aside some of the arbitrariness that we so often embrace.

Here is a short story that illustrates how the decisions made with Divine Agency must be in our favor and without ego. The truth is always larger than what the ego tries to protect, especially if the ego is motivated to harm others.

In Our Favor...

A sultan issued a decree: Any person who told a lie would be fined five dinars and sentenced to one day in jail. Up and down the crooked city streets, the town crier delivered the sultan's message to all. To test the people, the sultan disguised himself as a powerful but insignificant minister, and he traveled a short distance behind the town crier, just to be sure that everyone understood.

He stopped at the home of the wealthiest merchant and was invited in. The merchant, being a gentle host, offered the sultan the finest coffee, dates, and dried fruits. Wasting no time, the sultan asked the merchant three questions.

"How old are you?" asked the sultan.

"Thanks be to Allah, I have had 23 good years," replied the merchant.

"How many sons do you have?"

"I have one praiseworthy son," said the merchant.

"How much money have you accumulated?"

"Exactly eighty thousand dinars, all pledged in the name of Allah," answered the merchant.

The sultan thanked the merchant for his honesty and for his loyalty to Allah.

After checking the town record, the sultan was overjoyed with excitement. The merchant had been lying. Soldiers were dispatched to the merchant's house and a royal tribunal was established. The sultan presented his evidence. He said, "You told us you were 23 years old. The local records indicate you are 75 years of age. You said you had only one son; in fact, you have six sons. You said that your wealth totaled exactly eighty thousand dinars; however, you are the wealthiest man in the kingdom. How do you explain these discrepancies?"

The merchant replied, "You asked me how old I am and I answered with the total number of my good years, not the total of my good and bad years together. You asked me how many sons I have. I have one good son and five bad ones. My answer is truthful. My one son is the only one who worships with me, so I do not count the other five. You asked me how much money I have accumulated and I answered, 'Exactly eighty thousand dinars, all pledged in the name of Allah.' That is the amount of money I gave to build a mosque. That is the only wealth that matters to me. I did not answer with meaningless accumulation, but only with the most meaningful."

The sultan understood. Many evaluative measures can speak both to truth and to falsehood. If we speak the truth that is most in our favor to Allah or to ourselves, then it is truth. That way, the pain of loss is not ignored, and the fear that makes it hard for us to speak the truth can be set aside.

> Lost years, lost sons, and lost money are part of the relation we have, and if that is what is most truthful to us, that should not be taken from us. It must be acknowledged *first* before it can be set aside.[30]

The ME | NOT ME dynamic that organizes our pre-decisions often reveals what is most painful. One cannot change the impact of this pain if one has never borne the loss that makes the past so "real" to us. That's why Divine Agency, though uncommitted to any particular result, must always operate *in our favor*. The biblical adage, "Give unto Caesar what is Caesar's and unto God what is God's," illustrates a dynamic that cannot be set aside or placed under the power of someone else's perspective. If we are blind to the reality of loss, power will be needlessly destructive. Growth and transformation happen because we feel the privilege of favor. Our consent and acceptance of that must be acknowledged first; otherwise, we will feel powerless and unloved just as we are.

Zanshin Observation: The possible future that we discover in our contact with loss does not end with limitation. The future can be *in our favor* and without ego yet still uncommitted and open to any result, provided we are in the Zanshin Overlap.

30 (Modified). Based on the story, "A Higher Truth," by Nina Jaffe & Steve Zeitlin, *The Cow of No Color: Riddle Stories and Justice Tales from Around the World*, Henry Holt & Company, New York, 1998, pp 110-113.

Believers and Doubters

The 3D world of love and fear asks a lot of us. While our pre-decisions point to what we find most painful, they simultaneously reveal what is loving and healing for us. Like a movie audience, we can decide to be passive and accept the story that is told to us. But I would like to think the remaining mind motivates us to take greater responsibility, not less. Are we willing to do the interpretive work to challenge ourselves? It all depends on if we feel loved just as we are.

Some will, perhaps, question the growth and transformation that Divine Agency offers. To cast doubt on an idea that cannot be empirically measured seems both realistic and justified. But the unexamined assumptions that lie buried in our evaluation of the past make questions about growth and transformation difficult to avoid. What is permanent in one's life? What is temporary? Which impacts are irreversible and pervasive, and which ones can we endeavor to change? None of these questions can be answered definitively, and each accrues intensity primarily because we are so vulnerable and dependent on one another and on the story that is being told to all of us.

One potential definition for belief is "confidence." Are we confident that something is true? What creates confidence? Is it determined by a relation or by an outcome?

For example, if our loss is great, then we will be fearful and less open; confidence argues we *cannot* trust. If, on the other hand, we are optimistic and open to experience, here confidence argues that we *can* trust. The unfolding moment, when we assess it, causes us to be preferential, to see the world as one way or another. However, belief and doubt can turn on our willingness to share experience and to learn from one another, no matter the cost. Yet, as we know, this type of learning is supremely difficult achieve. We resist making confidence solely about others. So, Divine Agency uses consent and acceptance as the primary resources that enable us to reshape the ME | NOT ME dynamic. With consent and acceptance, confidence is not completely preferential. Here, we build new confidence by changing the story we tell ourselves but only by stepping away from the preferences that Personal and Impersonal Agency create. The target in the dark is our willingness to consent to whatever is needed—often with no guarantee at all.

A "belief system" is the values, traditions and principles that you live your life by. But how open will that be? The logic that Personal Agency brings to our belief system is the confidence that we place in how the gut rules the measure. The logic that Impersonal Agency brings is that evidence goes on without us so we are unnecessary. What Divine Agency offers is an opportunity to deepen the confidence that adds open—rather than closed-ended value, even as we shift the dynamic that captures and organizes our attention.

Ego, in the end, is the primary obstacle to greater flexibility; for with the Ego, protection, discernment and confirmation are judged to be integral to one overriding value that cannot be set aside.

Here is a short story that illustrates how we must be willing to alter the way we relate to our own experience.

Daybreak...or Nightfall?

A theology teacher asked his graduating class a final question: "How can you tell when nightfall has ended and daybreak begins?"

One student said, "When nocturnal animals crawl back to their lairs." Another said, "When the stars start to fade from the night sky." Still another said, "When no one misjudges the past by making it the present."

The teacher said, "You are all mistaken; however, the last answer is very close. It's when you look at the face of another person and you see them as a full human being. Because if you cannot do that, no matter what time it is, it is still night. You are, not yet, fully awake. The ego has robbed you of your ability to choose. [31]

Zanshin Observation: Belief and doubt hinge on our connection to others. Ego is the primary obstacle to greater flexibility because it limits (or distorts) confidence.

The Openness of the Remaining Mind

31 (Modified). Based on the story, "Signs of Daybreak," by Margaret Silf, *One Hundred Wisdom Stories from Around the World*, Lion Books an imprint of Lion Hudson, PLC, Oxford, England, 2003. p 86.

With a snap of the thumb, the openness of greater freedom can be yours.

Zanshin is about the *remaining mind*, the part that is waiting for us to set aside the normal preoccupations of life. That idea can be quite powerful. In the Eastern sense, it might be the doorway to a more enlightened spirit. In a Western sense, it might be the doorway to being more whole and complete just as we are. For each person, the task of becoming more zanshin will mean something slightly different. As we have seen, there are multiple variables at play in your life, long before you can focus your attention on any one of them—so the zanshin moment must precede what we generally regard as organized "reason." That's why we are so confused by indecision. It complicates the harmony we set out to achieve by undermining our confidence.

There are many causes for this confusion: incomplete information, lack of priority, conflicted feelings from the past, a misplaced sense of authority, an inability to find a natural fit between oneself and others. Personal Agency wrestles with each of these, often without success. The main tool of Personal Agency is its awareness of power and ego. We are invested in the utility of our decision since we are given full credit and full license to decide as we wish solely for the purpose of creating that which does not fully exist *as yet*. Perhaps it is that power which makes Divine Agency so transformative. If we let go of the ego's tendency to over-protect, over-discern or over-confirm, we come much closer to the true nature of dependence. Much like the bird that must run to take flight, the zanshin moment is a personal release from whatever we feel most acutely and painfully. We are dependent upon the air to carry us aloft when we, ourselves, did not put the wind beneath our wings. So the utility we find with Divine Agency cannot be conjured out of power and ego. Its utility can only be released by consent and acceptance for the relation *we are having*, which we must embrace for its own sake.

The tension between Impersonal Agency and Personal Agency is largely about discovery. If we make a decision and take action, in our mind's eye, what do we discover about ourselves? Divine Agency is about making *THE decision* to make that discovery; it's about being open enough to be different than we have been because there is something we are called to do which we know, unequivocally, we cannot let go of. Be that hope for the future, faith in a unified world, or the love we have for our friends, neighbors and family, *hope, faith and love* must have power over us, otherwise we are only relating to the ego and power of our self-created decisions.

What Divine Agency calls for is a slowing down and a deepening of the world so it might capture for us the essence of who we most want to become.

Here is a short story to that illustrates this ideal.

Essence or Image?

A wealthy man owned a priceless art collection. He proudly showcased his collection, knowing how it demonstrated his intelligence and finer sensibilities. This same man also had a much beloved son, and the two of them enjoyed giving tours of the art collection together.

However, war broke out. The son was called up to serve and he went overseas to fight. One day, the father received a telegram. His son had died in action. Devastated by the news, the old man grieved unremittingly. No one came close to capturing his heart the way his son did.

Several months passed and without warning, the old man received a knock at the door. A young man stood carrying a small package. He explained that he had served with the man's son overseas and that they had been great friends. He also said that it was he whom the son died trying to save. The young soldier was deeply in debt for his friend's courage and he drew a sketch of him. He said, "I'm not a great artist, but I knew that the two of you enjoyed art together, so I would like you to have this."

The father was silent for a long time. Looking at the picture, he was drawn to his son's eyes and how they looked back at him. He slowly started to cry. He thanked the soldier and offered to pay for the work. "Oh, no," said the soldier, "this is my gift. I have no way to thank your son for what he did. I want you to have this."

Time passed and the sketch was prominently placed over the mantel. Indeed, it became the old man's most favored work of art. No one toured the house without first being shown this sketch of his son. So deeply did it carry the son's imprint, nothing else seemed to matter.

Not long after, the old man died and his art collection went up for auction. Curators from around the world were ready to bid and it was likely that the collection would be scattered all over the world.

The auction booklet listed the sequence. The sketch of the son was the first picture up for auction. The curators complained that a work by such an unknown artist made no sense. The quality of the work was simply not up to the rest of the collection. The auctioneer tried to start the bidding, but no one was interested. He said to everyone in the room, "My instructions are clear, I must start with this painting first." Eventually, one hand went up. It was the maid who cleaned the house and who could remember the son before he died. "I'll give you $50 for the sketch." The hammer went down: Once, twice, three times. No other bids came from anywhere in the room. "Sold!" called the auctioneer.

And then, the auctioneer laid down his gavel. "The auction is over," he said. "My instructions from the deceased are clear. Whoever takes the first sketch receives the entire collection." [32]

Essence is a problem for ego. It's enlarging commitment to others frustrates the ego's desire to be seen in a certain way, either by our

---

32 (Modified). Based on the story, "The Auction," by Margaret Silf, *One Hundred Wisdom Stories from Around the World*, Lion Books an imprint of Lion Hudson, PLC, Oxford, England, 2003. pp 76-77.

decision or by what others decide. So once we finally do know what we "cannot let go of," essence ceases to be a neatly "defined" image at all. Like the riddle of the Sphinx, the mystery, itself, becomes the solution *and* the very next question that we are called upon to answer. Nothing truly settles the question, so we must continuously bring more of ourselves into the question itself. Interdependence is like that: a never-ending riddle that offers no solution. Duration, scope and preference are purely what you choose to make of them.

Zanshin Observation: The more we look at ego as something temporarily needed, the more we can place ourselves outside its demands. Essence precedes ego; not the other way around.

The Resilience Factor

One feature of Divine Agency is that it results in greater resilience. Resilience is a difficult quality to define, but for most, it is simply the ability to bounce back from hardship and adversity. The more the world resists, the more we are asked to bring forth the Core Essence that willingly chooses to connect to that which is larger than itself.

Consider the following riddle: What container has no lid, no bottom and a golden treasure tucked inside?

Before answering, consider how difficult resilience can be to achieve and how important it is. It's difficult because we *do* align with our goals; we see ourselves as part of what we hope to achieve. At the same time, the story being told to us is greater than the story we tell ourselves. Our resilience cannot be tied to any one outcome if our story is going to be larger than the one we tell ourselves.

The riddle's answer is *an egg*. The more we align with Divine Agency, and with the strength of Core Essence, the more we learn that our goals and aspirations have no lid and no bottom. We are able to be resilient because self-promotion is not the "end-all and be-all" of what we can accomplish. What unfolds in the Now can lead us to resilience, provided we are willing to find beauty in whatever happens. (Although car trouble never inspires this kind of reaction.)

Core Essence is to the individual what resilience is to the never-ending reality that surrounds us. Neither one ever quits. So when we are possessed by one agency *minus* the remaining mind, it's easy to feel like the frustrated driver who is "broken-down" by the car he wants to fix. The surest way to release that frustration would be for him to shift the focus of his attention. Zanshin patience is being larger than the temporariness of any one outcome.

The attributes commonly associated with resilience include[33]:

- **Spiritual orientation.** Resilient people often have a spiritual or religious orientation that helps to increase self-esteem, make and find meaning in life and improve family and other close relationships. Spirituality provides an effective moral

33 These are derived from several sources, so this list of attributes does not agree with any one specific source. For greater detail on resilience, see Reivich & Shatte, *The Resilience Factor: 7 Keys to Finding Your Inner Strength and Overcoming Life's Hurdles*, Three Rivers Press, 2002.

compass that helps individuals to navigate anxiety, stress and adversity without feeling put-upon in an arbitrary way.

- **An internal locus of control**. Resilient people believe that they, and not their circumstances, affected their achievements. They are the orchestrators of fate, not the recipients of it. In fact, on a scale that measured locus of control in one clinical experiment, resilient people scored more than two standard deviations away from the standardization group.[34]
- **A positive orientation and flexible reframing.** Resilient people meet the world on its terms by adapting as needed. They are autonomous and independent, they seek out new experiences and have a positive social orientation. Every frightening event, no matter how negative in appearance, has the potential to be traumatic or not to the person experiencing it. One of the central elements of resilience is perception; the more a frightening event can be reframed into something positive, the more resilient a person becomes.
- **Access to protective factors that support flexibility**. Traumatic stress and repeated exposure to adversity produces greater vulnerability. Protective factors help to mitigate and manage that vulnerability. Leading protective factors include strong bonds with others, concrete support in times of need, environmental stability, and a culture of diversity and tolerance.

Deciding how you will construe and explain adversity and its impact and seeing how that decision leads eventually to discovery and satisfaction are important sources of resilience. This is the primary way that Divine Agency engenders resilience for those seeking to be more zanshin.

This short story illustrates how resilience is both a thoughtful choice and a behavioral test. This story captures some of what being zanshin can be like if you are open to it.

---

34 These experimental results were covered by Maria Konnikova in *The New Yorker* article "How People Learn to Become Resilient" (February 11, 2016).

The Frog Who Wouldn't Give Up

Once upon a time, there were two frogs. One morning they were jumping up and down on the shiny, scrubbed floor of the farm's dairy.

The farmer's wife caught sight of these two frogs, and she took hold of a big broomstick to chase them out of the dairy. "I won't have dirty amphibians jumping up and down on my shiny dairy floor," she scolded.

In their panic, the frogs looked for somewhere to hide away, out of the range of the fearsome broom and the angry farmer's wife.

"Quick, over here," said one frog to the other. "I can see a hiding place where the broom will never reach us." So they hopped into a corner of the dairy, as fast as their froggy legs would carry them.

"Now jump, as high as you know how," said the first frog to the second.

So they jumped. High, and higher, and highest. They jumped higher than they had ever managed to jump before. They jumped right over the big, grey wall of the hiding place.

Plop! they landed, only to find themselves in a bucket of fresh cream, newly drawn off the milking pail.

"Oh dear," said the second frog to the first. "That's it! We're done for! No chance of getting out of here."

"Keep paddling," said the first frog. "There must be some way out. We'll think of something."

"But I'm so tired after all that jumping up and down," complained the second frog. "And I've completely exhausted myself making that great leap which landed me in this bucket. I haven't got any energy left to paddle around in a bucket of cream. It's no use," he croaked. "It's too thick to swim in, too thin to walk on and too slippery to crawl out of. We've had it. We're not going to get out of here alive." And with that, he gave up, sank down to the bottom of the bucket and died.

But his friend kept on paddling. He paddled all through the long, lonely, weary night. He often felt like giving up and joining his friend at the bottom of the bucket, but something made him keep on paddling.

To take his mind off his situation, he remembered a short rhyme:

Leap up my heart into the sky
And bring to me a butterfly
There's nothing here I do alone
When first I sit on lily throne.

Over and over and over, he repeated the rhyme. Eventually, the sun rose again, and the first beams of light came streaking across the dairy.

The frog who wouldn't give up looked down at the cream, tears of exhaustion welling up in his little froggy eyes.

To his amazement, he discovered that he was standing on a mountain of butter, which he had churned all by himself. [35]

The test we face is often unexpected. To invite a change doesn't mean we stop trying. We simply must look for the support and encouragement we can, knowing that the future is the result of both actions taken and luck. To bring insight, change and transformation to any decision, you must invite an inner engagement with your mind and heart, and you must also paddle furiously.

> **Zanshin Observation:** It's not enough to slow things down and be deliberate. There's always work to be done with every decision we make.

35 (Lightly modified). Margaret Silf, *One Hundred Wisdom Stories from Around the World*, Lion Books an imprint of Lion Hudson, PLC, Oxford, England, 2003, pp 149-150. I added the frog rhyme; that's all. Many versions exist on the Internet.

The Inconsistency of Partial Logic

It's one thing to be clad in the armor of our decisions; it's another to listen more closely to the story that is being told to you. In the first case, we are fully covered. Nothing gets in or out. In the second, we still "decide"—we're just resilient enough to let go of our more habitual defenses.

One reason why resilience is so important to decision making is that we often must confront the inconsistency of partial logic. Reason makes the evaluations that guide our decisions, while logic organizes and plans our various attempts to "make more" by "doing better." The life experience we have can make it seem that we must follow the "rational" evaluations (duration, scope and preference) of others, so it's not surprising that we often find ourselves in a conflicted or confused state. As with the suit of armor shown above, we must slowly pull apart individual pieces if we want to minimize the inconsistency of partial logic.

Recall the three examples of indecision that I introduced in Chapter 1: incomplete information, lack of priorities and conflicted feeling from the past. Our experience with indecision imposes costs, chiefly a decrease in the good feeling, self-image and level of confidence we normally have. All of these sources of strength are important, but just *how* important? The inconsistency of partial logic forces us to accept that we cannot arrive at a complete answer on our own. We are forced uncomfortably into partial disbelief in ourselves. Let us review the three examples.

1. **Incomplete Information**. A friend who has been having a difficult time at home and at work wants to meet with you, but does not give a specific time or place.

   Disbelief: You have no firm basis for a decision.

2. **Lack of Priority or Conflicting Priorities.** You can move to a new city to take a new job, or you can stay where you are and continue working where you have been.

   Disbelief: You cannot create fulfillment in advance.

3. **Conflicted Feelings from the Past.** Your current boyfriend is hedging his commitment to you, just like your old boyfriend did. You can decide the current situation is entirely different from the past, or you can think this might turn out just like that did.

   Disbelief: You cannot judge importance, past or present.

The inconsistency of partial logic creates unanticipated vulnerability and confusion. We struggle to make a clear decision when too much uncertainty remains. Our future course of action feels like the "unanswered ending," simply because we must wait and see what happens next. Each of the above situations makes us the primary "decider." So what do we do?

The "We'll See" Story

A poor farmer in the central region of China didn't have a lot of money, only an old horse to plow his field. However, his reaction to everything—no matter how good or bad—was always the same.

One afternoon, his horse dropped dead. Everyone in the village said, "Oh, what a horrible thing to happen." The poor farmer said, "We'll see."

The villagers, wanting to help, got together. They gave him a new horse as a gift.

Now, everyone said, "See, what a lucky man you are." The farmer said, "We'll see."

A few days later, that new horse jumped a fence and ran away. Everyone lamented, "How sad!" The farmer said, "We'll see."

Eventually, the horse found his way home. Everyone shouted, "What luck." The farmer said, "We'll see."

Later, the farmer's young boy went riding on the horse. He fell and broke his leg. The villagers all said, "How sad!" The farmer said, "We'll see."

Two days later, the army came into the village to draft new recruits, and because the farmer's son had a broken leg, they decided not to recruit him.

Who knows what may be good or bad? To everything, the farmer simply said, "We'll see."[36]

Zanshin Observation: We cannot see the whole game, nor can we see beyond the boundaries that we create. Be patient when cooperating with others.

If we give up a small degree of momentary confidence to gain a larger degree of lasting self-direction, we are being zanshin.

Reinforcing the SAFE Space of Being Zanshin

36 A popular and very old Zen Story.

Guilt and Fear do not get the last word. Reclaiming the openness of the remaining mind is always possible.

Divine Agency is about consent and acceptance. It is also about accessing inner support and encouragement. To reinforce the Stable, Adaptive, Flexible and Energized (SAFE) space of being zanshin, you must occupy the Zanshin Overlap. Sometimes decisions will come from direct contemplation (via Personal Agency), other times they will come from direct investigation (via Impersonal Agency), still other times they will come from patience and open-ended invitation (via Divine Agency). The more you can access the area of enhanced integration and interdependence (the Zanshin Overlap), the more you will be free of the ego's need to fix blame and cast doubt. If you can accept the space of not choosing to believe anything too narrowly or specifically, you can maximize your ability to be present and alert to all forms of potential and be more attuned to whatever might improve your situation.

Here's how to reinforce the SAFE space of being zanshin for each of the situations listed above.

1. **Incomplete Information.** With a situation that has too much missing information, there is always a desire to fill in the blanks. Making the decision to stop data-gathering is hard. So what do you do?
    a. Evaluate your perceptions and the information you have. What judgements and opinions are you making now (via Personal Agency)? Why are these important to you?
    b. Study your environment. What can you discover and learn about the people, resources and consequences that you did not already know (via Impersonal Agency)? Does this information create new opportunities?
    c. Be open to growth and transformation. If you get *no* additional information, can you make a decision anyway? By

inviting support and encouragement via Divine Agency, you can entirely change the way you are looking at your situation and begin operating in a different way from the past.

2. **Lack of Priority or Conflicting Priorities.** With a situation that has no priority or has only conflicting priorities, the future offers no clear reference. You must give yourself the room to explore where the greatest payoff might be, right now. So what do you do?
   a. Contemplate your perceptions by thinking about your judgements and opinions (via Personal Agency). Why do these have energy for you? Can you change how they feel?
   b. Look at your environment. What can you discover and learn about your priorities (via Impersonal Agency)? Is there something unexpected that might become your new priority?
   c. Be open to growth and transformation. If you assert a priority, then you must give up other priorities. By entreating support and encouragement (via Divine Entreaty), you might arrive at a novel solution, unlike anything you have tried in the past.

3. **Conflicted Feelings from the Past.** When a conflict arises from intense personal history, it's hard to know where to place your loyalties and which future will give you the most satisfaction. So what do you do?
   a. Evaluate the triggers that make this situation difficult for you. What judgements and opinions are you making (via Personal Agency)? Are these really still important to you?
   b. Study your behavior and the behavior of others. What can you discover and learn that you did not already know (via Impersonal Agency)? Is there an opportunity or an obstacle?
   c. Be open to growth and transformation. If you are still conflicted, can you make a decision anyway? If you find unexpected resources and use them in a new way, are you operating in a way that is substantially different for you?

Here is a short story that illustrates the importance of reinforcing the SAFE space of being zanshin.

Making Our Sukkah

Jewish tradition celebrates the harvest festival of Sukkot. The single most important custom of this holiday is to construct a small hut, called a *sukkah*, out in the open air. This commemorates the temporary structures that were made out in the desert as the Jews were escaping slavery. The open air is freedom and the temporary structure is like a small oasis. Each sukkah reinforces the idea that the God of Israel will provide His people a stable source of encouragement and support that will allow them to be adaptive, flexible and energized by the future ahead.

Jacob, a devoted Jew, brought his son, Nathan, out to his sukkah. He told him a story of a time long ago when he could not correctly say his prayers under his sukkah. Normally, the prayer begins with, "May it be Your will," said while holding the traditional prayer book. But that day, his prayer book had been left with his mother, so to make his words acceptable to God while standing under his sukkah, Jacob said, "Master of all, may it be Your will that it is *as if* I have said, 'May it be Your will.'" In sharing this story with Nathan, Jacob wanted his son to know that a devout heart is created by the way we offer what we have, even when that is less that what we might have wanted. Then he finished by saying, "May the words of my mouth be acceptable to You because in every prayer we always begin with 'May it be Your will.'"[37]

37 A hybrid story. The description of Sukkot festival comes from Nina Jaffe and Steve Zeitlin, *While Standing on One Foot: Puzzle Stories and Wisdom Tales from the Jewish Tradition*, Henry Holt and Company, New York, 1993, pp 81-92 and the rephrasing of the prayer opening comes from www.chalbad.org, a Jewish website. See http://www.chabad.org/holidays/JewishNewYear/template_cdo/aid/4511/jewish/The-Words-of-My-Mouth.htm

> **Zanshin Observation:** To be zanshin, we do not need a specific answer—just the willingness to make it to the other side of whatever happens. The more we can reinforce the SAFE space of being zanshin, the more we can bring its safety to all our choices and decisions.

Unanswered Endings

Incomplete information, lack of priority and conflicted feeling are the "unanswered" endings that can lead to indecision. We want the "fully answered" sense of clarity that reduces our isolation to satisfy our need for protection, discernment and confirmation. Yet, we cannot stop there. Accepting the requirement of patient waiting, as an engagement we want, must also offer us some satisfaction.

There have been multiple variables at play long before you could focus and attend to any one of them. Duration, scope and preference are filtered by experience and reflection. They do not "evidence" themselves. We must bring something of ourselves to them. Consequently, every change to orthodoxy is both challenge and opportunity.

The stories we tell ourselves, like some of the parables offered in this book, can potentially leave us hanging. The orthodoxy of our thinking, when personally or impersonally motivated, cannot be our sole and only appreciation for the story "being told to us." The gift of Divine Agency is the enormous help and assistance we actually *can* discover in the security that waiting offers. The beauty we find in the middle space of waiting is a deeper appreciation for compassion, gratitude and humility. Without them, equanimity and loving-kindness might never create our most prized gift: peace.

Inviting the inspiration and security that Divine Agency offers can bring new answers to unanswered endings without requiring any belief in a supernatural force.

No doubt you noticed: My association for the word "divine" is the heaven-like quality we create, and its fine to harbor a belief in a supernatural force provided it reinforces the prized gift of peace.

> **Zanshin Observation:** The fruit that our efforts bear for us cannot be measured by the logic we use. It's not about what we intend, even when we strive for integration and interdependence. Cooperation and patience surpasses whatever we can know in advance.

Indecision and Divine Agency

The skill of direct entreaty can be difficult because it requires an openness that often does not feel chosen. To exercise direct entreaty, you must be open to an indirect source that brings *to you* the insight, change and transformation which you might never choose for yourself. "Direct entreaty" is both an accurate label and somewhat oxymoronic.

The word "entreaty" means to request earnestly and urgently with a presence of mind that is as open as possible. For most of us, we slip into the behavior of direct entreaty when we are slowing down and deepening our appreciation of the world, so it may, then, capture and offer to us the essence of who we most want to become. This is the focus of many Eastern and Western meditative practices. It reinforces a willing patience and open-ended appreciation for whatever happens.

Remember the observations that have been made in this chapter:

- Let your decisions come through you but not from you. Be pure in heart and untroubled.
- Nothing prepares you for freedom but freedom itself. There is no self-promotion—only the Now.

- The possible future we discover in our contact with loss does not end with limitation. The future can be *in our favor,* without ego, and still uncommitted to any result.
- Belief and doubt hinge on our connection to others. Ego is the primary obstacle to greater flexibility because it limits (or distorts) our confidence.
- The more we choose to look at ego as something temporarily necessary, the more we can place ourselves outside its demands. Essence precedes ego, not the other way around.
- It's not enough to slow things down and be deliberate. There's always work to be done with every decision we make.
- To be zanshin, we do not need a specific answer—just the willingness to make it to the other side of whatever happens.
- We cannot see the whole game, nor can we see beyond the boundaries that we create. Be patient when cooperating with others.
- The fruit that our efforts bear cannot be measured by the logic we use. It's not always about what we intend. We cannot know everything in advance.

Personal Change and Direct Entreaty

Change is destiny. If you invite change, you can learn to participate with it. What change might be required if you were genuinely open? If you are struggling with an important decision and you cannot decide, might you entreat change by inviting a new type of fulfillment?

- Are you wishing for reconciliation or forgiveness? For a letting go or letting in of that which is feared or loved? For a reconnection to something long forgotten or a newfound courage in yourself and your purpose?
- If you could set asidc ego, what inspires you to faith, hope and love? Can you base your decision on that?

- If entreaty really involves YOUR unique being as someone who is blessed in the world, then which opportunities generate feelings of strength and resilience for you?

To practice consent and acceptance, consider the following intentions that may open the door to greater insight:

- What does this situation invite you to do?
- What pain would you like to have stop?
- What dream feels too big to let go of?
- Who are the people you might turn to for support and encouragement?
- If there is a higher power, what might that power say to you?
- Is reconciliation or forgiveness needed?
- If you were to let go of a fear or a love, which would it be?
- If you were to let in a fear or a love, which would it be?
- If you reconnected to something long forgotten, how would that change you?
- If you were to ask for courage for yourself, what would that look like?

Logic is how we seek after confirmation. The way you organize evidence leads to your appreciation of both risk and opportunity. Utility and our appreciation of it is a form of logic.

- Are you organizing evidence so that it generates action or inaction?
- If you take the Middle Path, might that desire for logically consistent confirmation be reduced? Can you patiently wait while drawing energy from an "impossible future"?

Appetite and spirit are the inner complements to a life well lived. If you are working at a gut level, then what appetite wants is concrete confirmation. The outcome is the preferred result that brings you to a new place. In contrast, what spirit wants is a fulfilling relationship and deepening trust. Here, the "enhanced" relation is the preferred result that brings you to a new place. The counterpoint created by appetite and spirit is that we want to be completely invested in both.

Avoidance, or more specifically the NOT ME planets in your personal galaxy, are more often than not, products of indecision. These often require special attention:

- Is there something you are avoiding because it feels like an obstacle? If so, identify it and entreat for encouragement and support.
- Do you feel pressured by limitation? If so, turn your attention towards opportunity instead.

Both of these unlock potential because they are focused on bringing to the forefront open-ended encouragement and support.

Direct Entreaty may prompt a shift in your decision making, especially if you are exhausted from using Direct Contemplation and Direct Investigation earlier. If so, you will feel the ease and confidence you need to move forward. If not, you have slowed down your exercise of agency and are nonetheless bringing forward new resources. Conflict is both an inner and outer reality that can imprison us if we feel vulnerable and threatened. Setting aside that fear by slowing down and deepening one's appreciation of the world is an important prerequisite for Divine Agency—a prerequisite that has the potential to offer back to you the essence of who you most want to become.

Here is a story that illustrates this principle.

Jackie's Choice

Jackie was frozen with fear. Her disappointment was too great. She felt betrayed by the inner workings of someone she trusted. "As soon as you trust yourself," wrote Goethe in the 1800's, "you will know how to live."

Jackie had been duped into believing that her husband would show up for an important meeting that couldn't advance without his input. Now, if Jackie had been completely truthful to her intuition, she knew that she was uncomfortable with this option. She knew he could not be trusted. Time and again, he had made it clear that his work and his schedule and his priorities were more important than hers. And while she generally was a compassionate person, she would never describe herself as someone who practices "idiot compassion"—that is, an earnest do-gooder's belief that everyone is trustworthy simply because compassion is such a "noble" sentiment. No, Jackie was usually discriminating, but since she also felt powerless, it was all that much easier to fall into denial.

The awareness that her husband was no longer the person she married had taken years to develop. Jackie loved him and the promise that started their relationship. She held fast to her ideal: marriage was for life. However, trust had to be shared and supported by genuine acts of help and love. Her husband simply felt too entitled by the status, prestige and money that his career offered. Jackie did not know if love and help had long disappeared into the helplessness created by his insistent workaholic behavior—but she knew something had to give.

That's where Jackie stands right now: frozen with fear at the crossroad of denial. And as soon as she took the first step to let go of her denial, tears came to her eyes.

She had so hoped that he wouldn't betray her, but that first moment of acknowledgement was itself a revelation. Sure, she was mad, but more importantly, she was in pain. Until she let that out, she could never discover the person she most wanted to become.

"As soon as you trust yourself, you will know how to live." Never had those words seem so true as they did as she stood alone in the corner of her lawyer's office. She was ready to make a new beginning. Something was changing the essence of who Jackie most wanted to become. Jackie would eventually come to love her husband in a new way, but it would also

> be a love that was wiser and more clear headed. Somehow she would find a way to help both of them, even though that change would cost her the memory of who she had tried to be—both for herself and for her husband.[38]

To some, this might not seem like an instance of Direct Entreaty. Jackie did not call out the name of a god, nor did she make any formal entreaty through prayer. But the act of standing vulnerable and open—in the face of great pain—is precisely what Direct Entreaty entails. When we do that, we are allowing that situation to change us forever and we are bravely facing the consequences by not distorting them. We are learning to find that essential place of trust—the one that always brings to us support and encouragement.

As mentioned earlier, Rumi wrote: "Beyond ideas of rightdoing and wrongdoing there is a field. I'll meet you there." Here is the one zanshin ideal that can carry you through all your decisions. Let that wisdom be a source of change and transformation.

What makes Direct Entreaty different from either Direct Contemplation or Direct Investigation is how we rediscover the need (and capacity) to renew trust in ourselves and others. Despite the worst that life can do to us, we can transform our understanding graciously, triumphantly and humbly.

If we are sewn into time by the pre-decisions we make about duration, scope and preference, then the stitching that binds us to experience and memory must be made entirely of elastic! I know THAT sounds funny, but I'm really quite serious.

Jackie made a presumption about her husband (and was more than a little persuaded by the helplessness of trying to change another person. We all know how hard that is!). If Jackie persisted in feeling helpless, she would never have had the capacity to confront her own pain. Every tightly sewn pre-decision is a place that Divine Agency

38 A purely invented story.

can change, as necessary, to support and encourage us. This is always done for our benefit, for our growth and transformation, because we *love the life we have despite the worse that life can do to us.* With Divine Agency, we are lifted out of helplessness and are given new life. Perhaps that smacks of an "authorized" belief or a catechism, but the point is that without the capacity to pull ourselves out of helplessness, we would never adapt to the interdependent life we *do have.* It's the reason why the utility pendulum swings both ways: nothing is completely fixed because it must be shared and discovered, just as our lives are shared and discovered—chaotically, haphazardly and almost entirely by trial and error.

Every person will confront and use Divine Agency in ways that are appropriate for him or her, but no one fully understands the rationale of concord and how it generates harmony and trust. Why? Because concord, itself, is dependent on a diversity of perspectives. We must gradually manage trust in ways that are forever open to change. The patient integrity that "shows up" as concord will always be hard won, because with every decision we make, we are shaping the person we most want to become. In the end, the confirmation of appetite (with its desire for concrete outcomes) is less critical to us than the relation which we must create for ourselves.

Spirit asks:

- Will *we* include ourselves in the very next moment because *we choose* to deal with the arbitrary in an inclusive way?
- Are we willing to live through a relation that can support us on both sides of whatever happens?

If we answer yes to both, then we are called to an *inter*dependent life. But it will never be easy. The logic of trust and connection is such that they must be broken if they are to be recast in a new way. Only by living now, in what must be a shared and interdependent moment, can we learn to set aside the inconsistency of partial logic.

Think of it this way. Trust leads to gratitude. Yet gratitude is subject to all the complexities of interdependent life. Were it not for the challenges, joys and sorrows we encounter—as loss, suffering and surrender—any appreciative awareness for hope faith and love would be meaningless and flat. The inconsistency of partial logic is how ego-driven it is. That inconsistency breaks open if we are openly, patiently and fully living in the Now. Then even in our pain beauty can break through.

As songwriter Leonard Cohen wrote, "There is a crack in everything; that's how the light gets in." Protection does not equate with discernment or with confirmation; *nor does* discernment, by itself, create an obvious protection or even a confirmation we must all willingly support. We never arrive at a wholly consistent form of logic—we must simply celebrate what we can share by living in the Now. There, we can be both "within ourselves" and "within others."

And that, truly, is life's greatest blessing.

Conclusion

Divine Agency is best developed along the midpoint of the Utility Pendulum.

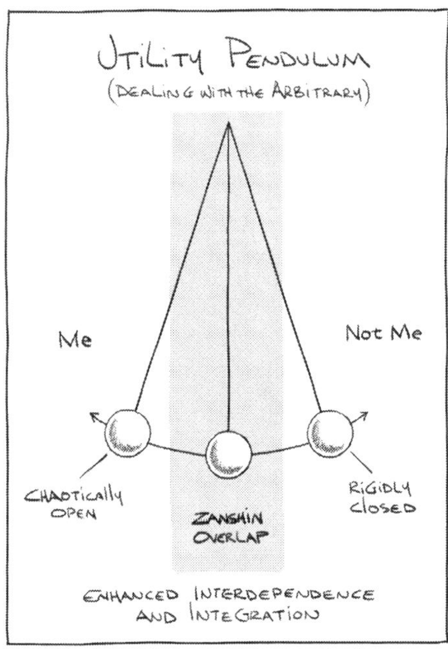

Divine Agency is *not* concerned with outcomes, nor with skills; it's concerned with consent and acceptance. Divine Agency asks us to look more closely at the person we want to become. The clarity that we discover with Divine Agency enables us to reset our perspectives and look past the burdens and limitations of *prior* experience. For each person, the revelation of Divine Agency will mean something slightly different. It may lead to reconciliation or forgiveness, a letting go or a letting in of that which is feared or loved, a reconnection to something long forgotten or a newfound courage in oneself and one's mission. All of these can reinforce our core sense of help and love—to "make more" by "doing better" with the life experience we have and to bring forward its promise every day.

Self-Help: Divine Agency

This chapter offered several insights that may help you negotiate the beliefs that make it difficult to focus on a preference that you want to advocate for yourself.

Directions: To complete the following, identify a situation that was difficult for you, then see if the topics introduced in this chapter might help you evaluate your situation in a new way.

Identify your problem situation here:

____

____

1. Flight Training

How likely is it that you believed the story you told yourself about your situation, rather than being part of how it unfolded?

Likely	**Not Likely**	**Unsure**
☐	☐	☐

2. What's 'Divine' about Divine Agency

How likely is it that you resisted compassion, gratitude and humility—if those emotions contradicted the story you were telling yourself?

Likely	**Not Likely**	**Unsure**
☐	☐	☐

3. Moving with the Now

How likely is it that you could drop your resistance and invite change so you could move more freely with the Now?

Likely	**Not Likely**	**Unsure**
☐	☐	☐

4. Believers and Doubters

If loss made you fearful and less open, how likely is it that you would trust others in a completely new way?

Likely	**Not Likely**	**Unsure**
☐	☐	☐

5. The Openness of the Remaining Mind

If the remaining mind allows you to set aside your normal preoccupations, would its greater flexibility be useful to you?

Likely	**Not Likely**	**Unsure**
☐	☐	☐

6. The Resilience Factor

If you could find something of beauty in whatever happens, would that appreciation be useful to you?

Likely	**Not Likely**	**Unsure**
☐	☐	☐

7. The Inconsistency of Partial Logic

If obstacles, pressures and fears make it difficult to focus on what *you* want, might the remaining mind release you from that?

Likely	**Not Likely**	**Unsure**
☐	☐	☐

8. Reinforcing the SAFE Space of Being Zanshin

If full credit and full license did not confirm what you wanted, how likely is it that the SAFE Space of being zanshin might open-endedly reset your entire way of seeing?

Likely	**Not Likely**	**Unsure**
☐	☐	☐

9. Confirmation as a Decision-Making Need

If Direct Entreaty is about maintaining a relation with "the story being told to us," is it useful to think of that relation as something we share with others as equal participants?

Likely	**Not Likely**	**Unsure**
☐	☐	☐

Conclusion

CONCLUSION

One agency *plus* the remaining mind, or one agency *minus* the remaining mind.

The difference sounds inconsequential, but if you are zanshin, the remaining mind will offer you more than what you expect. Where others are frustrated by the traffic jam, it is possible to float over the everyday concerns of time and limitation. The "Which Way?" signpost becomes a friendly reminder of how you want be more than you have been; not that you are now or ever have been less than you could be. Many people carry background beliefs that are difficult to let go of. Becoming zanshin can help them put aside the indecision of misdirected attention and repetitive anxiety.

One agency *plus* the remaining mind or one agency *minus* the remaining mind—the choice is yours.

Refocusing Our Efforts

The game show *Who Wants to Be a Millionaire?*™ illustrates the tensions commonly associated with decision making: the overwhelming need to take ownership of and then work through opportunity and risk, ecstasy and humiliation. What this game show also illustrates is how we are supremely drawn to outcomes that leave us better off than when we started. Why else do we fantasize about "winning" so much?

The purpose of this book is for you to realize *the power that is inside your decisions.* That power comes from choosing to be zanshin. Improving your decision making changes every aspect of your life and enables you to make more diverse decisions—not because "winning" is your primary goal, but because you can use the zanshin remaining mind to "make more" by "doing better" with everything you have. The more you place your attention in the Zanshin Overlap, the easier it will be to access the power of being zanshin.

Zanshin is a state of awareness that is open, uncommitted, and relaxed. When you are zanshin, you possess open-ended possibility. That access allows you to become more than you have been. Your ability to discover and then act on the full spectrum of fulfillment is vastly improved.

Summarizing the Remaining Mind

The remaining mind is the latent ability to anchor one's decision making across conflicting points of view, even those that might run counter to one's immediate interests. It's why one agency *plus* the remaining mind is better than one agency *minus* the remaining mind.

Where Personal Agency combines reason, logic, appetite, and spirit so we can be committed *to* and invested *in* a preferential feeling, Personal Agency is also limited by that feeling. The remaining mind allows you to shift focus and release that preferential feeling. With Impersonal Agency, you are on a quest to better understand the relation you are having, without really trying to shape that relation in any specific way. The remaining mind draws you closer into that relation and gives you the insight to see opportunities that you never considered. Divine Agency asks us to look more holistically at what is "personal" about our preferential feeling. Can we be more than we have been? Are we willing to change? Here, the remaining mind resets the ME | NOT ME dynamic, so Personal Agency no longer organizes the ME | NOT ME dynamic in the same way.

The remaining mind is the inner essence that can surpass one's defaults and even the sum total of past experience to offer a picture of one's self that he/she otherwise would *not have*. It is a love that remains with us *and for us* despite the worst that life can do. It is a love and a mystery that surpasses all understanding.

Decision Making Matters

As a Certified Financial Coach™, I see firsthand that what goes into a financial decision is pretty dry: revenues, expenses, rates of return, taxes, and cash flow planning. Yet most people are both fascinated by the power of money and also completely turned off by it. It seems so incredibly arbitrary that we're not sure how to relate to it. And that is precisely why this book is so necessary. Nowhere does the double-drawn portrait of risk and opportunity present itself so clearly as with financial choices and decisions. Risk and opportunity are personally constructed reflections of how we choose to meet the world—a world that is, unquestionably, larger than ourselves. A financial decision is always "you" against that much larger "system," a system that cannot make any personal assessment on your behalf. With financial decisions, you are truly on your own because *only you* can decide *what is enough*. Will you risk the good feeling, self-image and confidence you have right now to realize an unknown improvement by stepping across the decision-making threshold? It takes practice, support and a willingness to risk. When you do take a financial risk, it is because you are willing to land on the other side by accepting either a positive or negative result. You are choosing the relation—not the result. You are deciding to be in the center of the Zanshin Overlap.

The enigma of "enough" relative to the arbitrary "system" we face is that if we want to include ourselves on the other side of our decision, it is not the "system" that limits and controls us; it is the way we choose to see one another. Can you risk the good feeling, self-image and confidence you have right now and see others as your equal, and not as representatives of a "system"?

Behavioral Economics and Betrayal Aversion

An interesting study was done in behavioral economics[39] regarding an individual's willingness to trust others. The goal was to compare the degree to which a person would prefer to trust another person (who may or may not act as expected) rather than nature (which would only act in a random or arbitrary way). The consistent result was that we are more willing to trust nature than we are to trust one another. In the parlance of the study, we are "betrayal aversive." Nature may be random, but there is no personal edge to what nature does. There is, however, a personal edge to how we are treated by others.

Behavioral economists theorize that betrayal aversion is about "asymmetric information." People are by nature, risk aversive, preferring to maintain the status quo rather than take unnecessary risks with the good feeling, self-image and confidence they have right now. Risk aversion is a well established behavioral response. We don't want to lose anything. Betrayal aversion is *inter*personal risk. Similar, but different. If someone holds information that you do not have, are you willing to trust them to act as you would expect or prefer? Unavoidably we will find that from time to time, our trust *is* betrayed because people act on information that we, personally, do not have.

---

39 The study was done by Birnberg and Zhang (2010), "When Betrayal Aversion Meets Loss Aversion: The Effects of Changes in Economic Conditions on Internal Control System Choices," *Journal of Management Accounting*, December 2011.

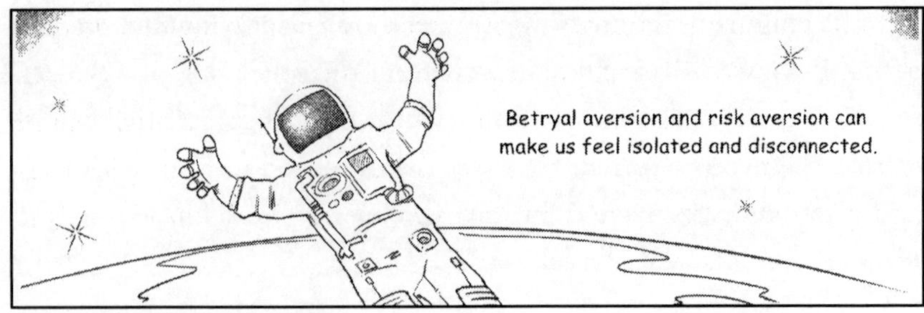

The forward momentum of life rejects the detailed understanding of the backward glance. Betrayal aversion and loss aversion have the potential to make us feel adrift without an anchor simply because our understanding (meaning everyone's understanding) is asymmetric. The backward glance is only marginally useful when others have completely different backgrounds and experience.

So the question is, what are we willing to do about that? The three agencies are guideposts that can help us.

If you are at risk of betrayal, can you exercise **Personal Agency**? Can you think more carefully about what is at stake? Which of the available options holds the most risk? Are you being pushed into a situation or thrown out of it? Do you have a presumption about what you expect to see happen? Are you looking for a specific confirmation of these as a specific outcome?

The more you are able to work through these questions on your own and bring optimism, the less you will need to place your energies out on the extremes of the Utility Pendulum.

Equally, if you are at risk of betrayal, can you exercise **Impersonal Agency**? Can you investigate more directly what is going on? Can you take an impartial, hands-off approach? Can you use enthusiasm, curiosity, empathy and imagination to test out what is going on? What kind of feedback exchange is going on? Is someone placing themselves as "one up" or "one down" to you? Are they shutting down the feedback for no reason?

The more neutral you are, the more you can work through the decision-making risk by bringing attention to unrecognized people, resources and consequences. Most likely, however, that will only happen if you are SAFE and in the Zanshin Overlap.

Finally, if the risk of betrayal is *unavoidable* (or has actually come to pass), can you let go of your ego investment? Are you willing to be larger than the situation itself? The goal with **Divine Agency** is to give yourself *some place to be* on the other side of what happened. The pain of betrayal is how it alters your good feeling, self-image and confidence. Restoring that requires you to look past the isolating power of Personal Agency. With Divine Agency, we must ask the questions that will prompt us to reconsider the good feeling, self-image and confidence we had previously so we may re-establish that awareness without burdening others or being too dependent on them for our well-being.

- What does this situation invite you to do?
- What dream feels too big to let go of?
- If there is a higher power, what might that power say to you?

Only the remaining mind can help you with these questions.

Arbitrary Systems Will Betray Us

With *inter*dependence, betrayal is inevitable. You would never grow if you did not experience the pain of betrayal and receive its opportunity to teach you and lead you to a new place of discovery. The trigger preferences of ME | NOT ME are vast reservoirs of personally digested experience that help you locate yourself in the context of an arbitrary system that offers both opportunity and risk. Being zanshin expands your awareness for both.

We can never be completely equal to an arbitrary system. We fantasize about winning because every loss feels like a betrayal. We ask ourselves, "What is enough? If I cannot extend trust to others, then can I at least extend trust to myself?" The asymmetry of information makes it hard for us to be "whole" on the other side of the decisions we make. We are risk aversive and betrayal aversive because we are not omniscient, immortal, and omnipotent. Vulnerability is the intersection of opportunity and risk. When we are most vulnerable, it is because the good feeling, self-image and confidence we have asks more from us than we are willing to give—at least not without resilience or courage. To move in the direction of a relation that leaves us better off than we started, we cannot measure everything by its result. We must turn to ourselves and one another, for at least there, we *genuinely* can "make more" by "doing better."

It's undeniable that we live in a very complex time. The choices and decisions we face seem almost insurmountable: climate change, global economies, genetic discoveries, scientific progress, and information overload. Complexity forces us to simultaneously confront so many realities that we cease trying to make any judgement at all, other than to feel the pain of our loss. How do we participate in a larger, interdependent world, when there is so much to "know" and so little time to invest in understanding how everything works? We feel entirely dependent on others. How do we ask an arbitrary system to make a personal assessment on our behalf? We cannot. The best we can do is to hold one another accountable to the loss that we feel. That way, we will continue to have one another to offer encouragement and support—provided we can stay in the center of the Zanshin Overlap.

The chaos of complexity is how much it scares us into thinking that we don't know how to live together on this one small planet. With the earth's population exceeding seven billion people today, the pressure of collective appetite makes it harder and harder to look past the national, cultural, economic, and environmental separations. The monumental and arbitrary forces are pushing their way into the tent. It is becoming more difficult to share cooperatively across all these separations. Our default response is to emphasize the independence of our identities and to deny the arbitrary consequence that nobody chooses to acknowledge explicitly. We are less empowered whenever denial and separation become our primary relation. You are either for me or against me. It's either my way or the highway. The economics of choice and confirmation make it hard to integrate ambiguity. To eventually learn how the "good" and "bad" breast are a part of the same mother figure is not an economic dance, it is a spiritual one.

Turn, Bend and Twist

Joseph Campbell had a very simple hope: the mythic promise that drives us forward is our willingness to integrate ambiguity and this might, perhaps, someday offer us some degree of resolution from insurmountable complexity. It is a hope worth considering.

Campbell outlined the three stages of the mythic journey: Initiation, Departure and Return.

- *Initiation is separation.* We must place ourselves into a reality that is not of our making. We must sense how it has the potential to change us. We must turn our attention to that so we can understand the nature of the problems we face. Initiation is somewhat like Direct Contemplation. We acknowledge our separation by examining the reason, logic, appetite and spirit that causes us to identify with our separation.
- *Departure is setting aside that separation.* We must put aside the more pronounced emphasis we give to our individual and personal perspectives so we can create new solutions. Departure is somewhat like Direct Investigation. We must be hands-off and use enthusiasm, curiosity, empathy and imagination to learn more about others and about the arbitrary system that knows more than we do. Here we must *bend* the personal to become more impersonal.
- *Lastly, return is the transformation of the personal.* Here we return to where we started. To quote T.S. Eliot: "We shall not cease from exploration. And the end of all our exploring will be to arrive where we started and know the place for the first time." Return is somewhat like Direct Entreaty. We change the nature of the personal so that our capacity for good feeling, self-image and confidence are renewed. Here we must *twist* the person we once were, to become someone new.

Enthusiasm, curiosity, empathy and imagination are, perhaps, more needed now than ever before. But if we think this investigation is about manipulating or changing our natural environment rather than one another, we might be fooling ourselves. We owe it to the silent spring of our awakening (the future generations that will follow after us) to do something that can enable life to be diverse and rich, not just now, but in the future as well. To deal with complexity and with the asymmetry of information, we must find new ways to turn, bend and twist the identifications that drive the ego to be more limited than it need be. We must practice the long-term way of relating, which Reinhold Niebuhr spoke of when he wrote:

> *Nothing worth doing is completed in our lifetime; therefore we must be saved by hope. Nothing true or beautiful makes complete sense in any immediate context of history; therefore we must be saved by faith. Nothing we do, however virtuous, can be accomplished alone; therefore, we are saved by love.*

The more we can identify with the ideal that is being expressed here, the more we can separate from the defaults that make the ego more important than our choosing to survive together. What the ego never knows and what the remaining mind always knows, is when our striving is excessive and when it is enough.

The Zanshin of Enough

Lynne Twist in her book, *The Soul of Money: Reclaiming the Wealth of Our Inner Resources*, wrote:

> *When you let go of trying to get more of what you don't really need, it frees up oceans of energy to make a difference with what you have. When you make a difference with what you have, it expands.*

The zanshin of enough is how we generate that feeling of expansion. The more open we are to how the remaining mind shifts our attention, the more easily we will know when our striving is enough. To twist, then, on that recognition opens the door to a future that may be our “target in the dark.” That future may well be larger than some of us can imagine. That’s why leadership is so important.

We can never tell whether another person is being zanshin, so making some evaluation of “enough” is the best we can hope for. Courage and altruism are indicators, but perhaps not definitive markers. Our evaluations are both hidden and subjective. Asymmetric information is hard to avoid. Still courage, like altruism, takes a personal risk so that someone else might benefit, and to my way of thinking, the expansion of the remaining mind requires risk taking but always as open-ended opportunity.

The unanswered ending we face is how the future continues to unfold. The zanshin of enough gives us permission to fail and to succeed, so long as we remain open and connected. Here is a final story that might underscore that idea.

The Stranger’s Gift

There once was a village that had fallen into fear. The villagers had been happy, kind and hospitable—famous for their friendliness and welcoming to everyone who passed through.

But anxiety and fear had taken over. The villagers fought and quarreled, almost for no reason. Rivalries sprang up. Where once there had been friendship and trust, now there was conflict and deceit. Everything about the village was clouded by uncertainty and the overhang of blame and mistrust.

The village elder was deeply saddened. He cried for the village and its future. “How will we get along?” he asked. He could do nothing to change it. Strangers no longer visited. The people no longer cared about the village, so eventually it fell into ruin.

But it happened that one day a stranger passed through, entering the village square as if he already knew about the people who lived there. Soon, he met the elder.

The elder told the stranger about his sadness and despair and how much he longed to see the villagers return to their kindness and trust. The stranger told the elder that he knew a way to redeem the lost community and to restore it again. The elder was curious. "I've tried everything," he said. "Tell me your secret."

The stranger said, "I will. But you must be brave, take risks, and blame no one." The elder agreed.

"First, you must be brave, for it will require courage to release the fear that is running through your village." The elder agreed, "Yes, yes. Bravery will be required."

"Next," the stranger said, "you must take a risk—you must do something that has never been done before." Leaning in, the elder asked, "And what is that?" The stranger touched his shoulder and said, "When the time comes, you will know."

The stranger added quickly, "No one can know beforehand what risk must be taken, but promise me when the time comes, you will take that risk." Feeling he had no choice, the elder reluctantly agreed, "Yes, I will."

"And finally," the stranger continued, "you must not blame the one person in the town who has not yet intervened to help." Now the elder became especially curious, "Who? Who has not intervened?"

The stranger said, "The one true leader, the one who was foretold long, long ago." The village held a traditional belief that all strife would be cured by the arrival of the one true leader. Understanding this, the elder became even more excited, "Do you mean he is here? He is here with us?" "Yes," said the stranger. And, with that, the stranger left just as quickly as he had come.

The elder was beside himself. This stranger had an air of authority about him that was irrefutable. "The one true leader is already here?" The elder considered the implications of telling anyone. "This might be a risk, but the news seems too important," he thought. So he told just one other person, his closest friend, but that was enough. The rumor spread across the village like wildfire. Everyone was asking themselves, who is the one true leader? Who is the person who should be held

> blameless? And because no one really knew for sure, the idea that he might be there among them already made them see things differently. Might it be the shopkeeper? Or how about the tailor? Or the woman who helps the children in school? The speculation was unending.
>
> But the funny thing was, after the stranger's visit, everyone in the village became braver, they started to take risks and they were committed to holding one another blameless. Almost overnight, the town went from blame and mistrust to a quiet reverence and regard. They started to live like people with one common purpose and with every encounter they asked themselves, "Might this be the one true leader?"—not knowing for sure if the answer would be "Yes."
>
> Before long, visitors came back. The old reputation returned. Friendship and trust took over. There was a happy, almost even holy, atmosphere of equality and trust. The stranger never came back. Why would he? There was nothing left to do.[40]

The community we share with those who happen to be familiar and close to us, need not be *the only* community to which we belong. The asymmetry of experience we share with them need not be arbitrarily imposed on others simply because they happen to be of our family, clan or tribe. The uniqueness of that which has been bestowed upon us individually, to each and every one of us is, by itself, enough. We need only courage to recognize that.

You are *to you*, the personal, permanent and pervasive source of all your experience. The more you can live that, the more you can share that with others.

Yes, we know that Ego protects, Experience discerns, Core Essence confirms. We want and can have protection, discernment and confirmation. Accept your desire for that and embrace your

40 (Lightly modified). Based on a traditional wisdom story. See 'The Stranger's Gift' in *One Hundred Wisdom Stories from Around The World*, by Margaret Silf, Lion Books an imprint of Lion Hudson, PLC, Oxford, England, 2003, p 131.

ability to accentuate and build upon the maybe. Indecision no longer cripples you or has you in its grip or takes away your power. Nothing takes away your power.

The power inside your decisions is you.

You are more than you have allowed yourself to be. Until now. Step into the power of being zanshin.

Humor is especially zanshin. To see what is funny in our lives requires the remaining mind to bring forward new and surprising perspectives.

You are most zanshin when you feel the source of your agency and when you are participating with that source. Then the remaining mind becomes a compatriot and counterfoil. The surprise is that we can see two things at the same time (but only when we are willing).

The cover design illustrates three koi fish. Good feeling, self-image and confidence are always swimming in a dance around some aspect of nature. We want to be more like nature but instead are drawn to be more like one another. The social and the natural are held in a magnetic and mysterious relation that, hopefully, supports and sustains us over our lifetimes.

The koi fish design offers you a way to think about shared participation and what it means to be in community.

There's nothing here I do alone
When first I sit on lily throne.

The flower of enlightenment is, for most of us, a complex devotion to community and what it might offer.

Zanshin: The Summary "Tutorial"

So you are facing a tough decision. What do you do?

- Look first to what has your attention. Why is this decision a tough one? Not enough information? Mixed priorities? Past experience?
- What is the *one* thing that creates the most ambivalence? The potential of being judged? The uncertainty of the outcome? The amount of coordination required?
- Now that you have a handle on your decision ambivalence, see if you can adopt a neutral outlook so you can explore it in a more directed way.

Personal Awareness and Direct Contemplation

Your thoughts and motivations come from reason, logic, appetite and spirit. Any ambivalence means that you are holding different perspectives about your decision. Ask specific questions of each perspective.

Reason: What have you already decided about the situation? If you identify the duration, scope and preference, you may uncover potential options.

- You have a preference—what is that? Are you personally put into the situation or thrown out of it?
- You are forecasting a duration. (How permanently charged is this?) Do you feel conflict here?

- You are forecasting a scope. (How pervasive is the relevance?) Do you feel conflict here?

Logic: How are you organizing that? Is it leading you to action or inaction? Are you limited by evidence and a need for confirmation?

Appetite and Spirit: Is there something you might be avoiding that feels like an obstacle? If you are feeling the pressure of limitations, see if you can identify opportunities instead.

Decision ambivalence points to inner conflict. Direct Contemplation is useful if you are aware of that conflict and if you want to uncover why your ambivalence is stopping you.

If Direct Contemplation does not offer any new decision alternatives, hold the information you have lightly and shift into using Impersonal Agency.

Personal Action and Direct Investigation

Become an impartial observer. How can you gather more information about your situation?

- Use enthusiasm, curiosity, empathy and imagination. If your situation is like a black box and you know nothing about the people, resources or consequences, how might you relate differently to it?
- Be an impartial spectator to your negotiation of feedback and to all the various elements that seem unknown to you. If you are not concerned with any outcome, how would you like to engage with the people, resources, and potential consequences? Can you remain impartial when the situation feels unknown?
- From this new perspective, what stands out as your potential opportunity? This is an opportunity that only you can realize. Can you identify a potential course of action that wasn't available to you previously?

Direct Investigation is built on *a desire to explore the relation you are having* rather than making a specific decision right away. If Direct Investigation does not offer any new decision alternatives, put that wish for alternatives out in front of you and give it your full attention. Now allow Divine Agency to come forward and see if the person you most want to become can open up a new way of relating.

Personal Change and Direct Entreaty

Change is destiny. If you invite change, you can participate with it. What change might be required if you decided to fulfill the intention of "making more" by "doing better"? Can you entreat a change by inviting a new type of fulfillment?

- Are you wishing for reconciliation or forgiveness? For a letting go or letting in of that which is feared or loved? For a reconnection to something long forgotten or a newfound courage in yourself and your purpose?
- If you could put your ego aside, what insight inspires you with hope?
- If this really is YOUR potential opportunity, which parts generate feelings of strength and resilience?

Now, you are ready to decide. Your decision will no longer be simply a reflection of a single-point focus (which is what your ego generates).

- If you are indecisive due to lack of information, you will be willing to accept the risk.
- If you are indecisive due to changing priorities, you will offer one alternative as a place of opportunity.
- If you are indecisive due to a conflict with the past, you will have new strength to be more than you have been.

The First Decision

For each agency, the First Decision is the most instrumental:

- Will you rationalize your situation through a model of interpretation that causes you to feel or think in a specific way?
- Or will you include yourself in the very next moment by being inclusive of whatever happens?

Good feeling, positive self-image and a high level of confidence are more open to change than we care to admit. If you free-fall to a new place, universal love *will* catch you—you can count on it!

Sources

I cannot list every source that inspired me, so let me just hit the most important ones.

Peter L. Bernstein. *Against the Gods: The Remarkable Story of Risk.* New York: John Wiley & Sons, Inc., 1996.

An encyclopedic look at opportunity and risk. The author evaluates the earliest notions of how risk can be quantified and how all our attempts to quantify risk fall short of providing us with the assurance we crave. Insightful and highly readable.

Chabris, Christopher, and Daniel Simons. *The Invisible Gorilla: How Our Intuitions Deceive Us.* New York: Broadway Paperbacks, 2009.

A fascinating book about the prevalence of bias in our perceptions. The author surveys attention, memory, confidence, knowledge, cause and potential as six areas of bias. Firmly a dis-believer in intuition, the author assumes that the best that intuition can do is connect us with our own reflection. Knowledge, if it is to have credibility, must be taken out of the realm of intuition.

Malcolm Gladwell. *Blink: The Power of Thinking Without Thinking.* Boston: Back Bay Books / Little, Brown and Company, 2005.

A delightful book about the power of intuition in organizing our judgements and perceptions. Gladwell explains how experience informs the subconscious so our judgements about complex subjects can be arrived at on the basis of small amounts of information. "Thin-slicing" information as a means for generating spontaneity is an important factor in how we learn to trust ourselves and the world around us.

William Glasser, M.D. *Positive Addiction*. New York: Harper & Row, 1976.

An older book that examines the importance of "positive" addictions. The author argues that people can change themselves by becoming addicted to positive behavior, such as exercise or meditation. By emphasizing the importance of positive activities, people can overcome weakness, anxiety and stress. The more positive we are in our habits, the more we can affirm the overlap of self-esteem and strength. The author's observations led me to believe that cooperation is a positive addiction that can be sustained and supported with the right outlook.

Hanson, Rick, Ph.D., with Richard Mendius, M.D. *Buddha's Brain: The Practical Neuroscience of Happiness, Love & Wisdom.* Oakland, Calif.: New Harbinger Publications, Inc., 2009.

An important book about neuroscience and the non-attachment of Buddhist practice. The author traces several Buddhist principles and identifies why they work in supporting our engagement with the world. He then explains how neuroscience can support and explain the effects Buddhist principles have. Regulate, learn and select; first dart / second dart; and equanimity are a few concepts presented with insightful vigor and conviction.

Donna Hicks, Ph.D. *Dignity: Its Essential Role in Resolving Conflict.* New Haven: Yale University Press, 2011.

A masterful examination of the abstract concept of "dignity" and how it affects conflict. Hicks' ten elements of dignity include:

acceptance of identity, inclusion, safety, acknowledgment, recognition, fairness, being given the benefit of the doubt, empathetic understanding, independence and accountability. Dignity outlines critical ideas with regard to cooperative behavior. Cooperation without dignity may be possible, but it will never be affirming to either side.

Robert Holden. *Shift Happens*. Carlsbad, Calif.: Hay House, Inc., 2011.

A short, succinct book about personal transformation. More anecdotal than research-based, the book examines how the "Unconditioned Self" is every person's original potential and how, through real-world conditioning, we wind up turning that original potential into self-doubt, self-criticism and self-attack. A powerful demonstration of our need for positive belief and a stronger spiritual orientation.

Jean Houston. *A Passion for the Possible: A Guide to Realizing Your True Potential*. New York: Harper Collins, 1997.

An evocative new-age book that encourages passion and commitment. This four-level examination includes: the sensory world, the psychological realm, the mythic journey and the spiritual quest. The book consistently affirms that every person is more than his or her past experience. The Daimon (or Inner Perceiver) concept originated here.

Marco Iacoboni. *Mirroring People: The Science of Empathy and How We Connect with Others*. New York: Picador, 2009.

An excellent, early book about mirror neurons and how they influence our social behavior and judgement. Icaboni argues that connecting to others is largely about connecting to the history we have and to the image-making that is primarily intuitive and pre-conscious.

Kegan, Robert, and Lisa Laskow Lahey. *Immunity to Change: How to Overcome It and Unlock the Potential in Yourself and Your Organization.* Watertown, Mass.: Harvard Business Review Press, 2009.

A recent book about how hard it is to change. The authors develop a "four-column" tool that looks at: commitments, behaviors, competing commitments and assumptions. What makes it so difficult for us to change is our competing commitments and the big assumptions that we carry about ourselves without our awareness, just to keep those competing commitments in place. The dynamic of immunity is explained as a conflict between "the knowing system" that organizes reality and "the feeling system" that manages anxiety. Both sides can create an immunity to change, because knowing and feeling are intertwined.

Reivich, Karen, Ph.D., and Andrew Shatte, Ph.D., *The Resilience Factor: 7 Keys to Finding Your Inner Strength and Overcoming Life's Hurdles.* New York: Three Rivers Press, an imprint of Crown Publishing Group, 2002.

The best book on resilience I have read. While it does cover a lot of material, it manages to distill it into a manageable message: *You can develop resilience through accurate thinking.* It is not that we are a "believing" species, but that we are a "self-correcting" species that actively chooses to look at the long term. The best part of the book is its relatively short description of explanatory style. When bad (or good) things happen, the explanation for "what" happened is consistently translated into terms that are Personal, Pervasive and Permanent. This one insight was the primary impetus for my book.

Daniel J. Siegel, M.D. *Mindsight: The New Science of Personal Transformation.* New York: Bantam Books, 2010.

A combination of psychotherapy practice and brain science, the book uses clinical stories to demonstrate the importance of personal transformation. Defined as integration of "the self" across eight domains, transformation is a tripod of reflection: openness, observation and objectivity, which result in a compassionate state of mind. Implicit and explicit memory concepts and abundance, acceptance, kindness and peace as the outgrowth of mindful reflection were all inspired by this book.

Nassim Nicholas Taleb, *The Black Swan: The Impact of the Highly Improbable*. New York: Random House, Inc., 2007.

An eclectic examination of uncertainty and our inability to identify its sources. The author weaves together both popular perspectives and statistical perspectives to offer the reader an unvarnished appreciation for what he calls Black Swan events, random moments of uncertainty that change everything and that come entirely out of the blue. Very entertaining and insightful.

Wisdom Story Sources (not in alphabetical order)

Jaffe, Nina, and Steve Zeitlin. *The Cow of No Color: Riddle Stories and Justice Tales from around the World.* New York: Henry Holt and Company, 1998.

Jaffe, Nina, and Steve Zeitlin. *While Standing on One Foot: Puzzle Stories and Wisdom Tales from the Jewish Tradition*. New York: Henry Holt and Company, 1993.

Margaret Silf. *One Hundred Wisdom Stories from Around the World.* Oxford, England: Lion Hudson, PLC, 2003.

Dr. Jorge Bucay, PhD. *Let Me Tell You A Story: Tales Along the Road To Happiness.* New York: Europa Editions, 1999.

Pulsifer, Catherine and Byron Pulsifer. *Inspirational Words of Wisdom.* http://www.wow4u.com/stories

John Suler. *Zen Stories to Tell Your Neighbors.* http://users.rider.edu/~suler/zenstory/zenframe.html

Chade-Meng Tan. *What Do You Think, My Friend?: Writings On Buddhism.* http://www.whatdoyouthinkmyfriend.com/Stories/index.html

JainWorld.com. *Jainism Global Resource Center.* see http://www.jainworld.com/literature/strindex.htm

Made in the USA
Middletown, DE
12 January 2017